Crucible of Resistance

CRUCIBLE OF RESISTANCE

Greece, the Eurozone and the World Economic Crisis

Christos Laskos and Euclid Tsakalotos

PlutoPress
www.plutobooks.com

First published 2013 by Pluto Press
345 Archway Road, London N6 5AA

www.plutobooks.com

Distributed in the United States of America exclusively by
Palgrave Macmillan, a division of St. Martin's Press LLC,
175 Fifth Avenue, New York, NY 10010

British Library Cataloguing in Publication Data
A catalogue record for this book is available from the British Library

ISBN   978 0 7453 3381 6   Hardback
ISBN   978 0 7453 3380 9   Paperback
ISBN   978 1 8496 4951 3   PDF eBook
ISBN   978 1 8496 4953 7   Kindle eBook
ISBN   978 1 8496 4952 0   EPUB eBook

Library of Congress Cataloging in Publication Data applied for

This book is printed on paper suitable for recycling and made from fully managed
and sustained forest sources. Logging, pulping and manufacturing processes are
expected to conform to the environmental standards of the country of origin.

10   9   8   7   6   5   4   3   2   1

Typeset from disk by Stanford DTP Services, Northampton, England
Simultaneously printed digitally by CPI Antony Rowe, Chippenham, UK and
Edwards Bros in the United States of America

To Evi and Heather

Contents

Acknowledgments

This book develops many of the themes of our two previous books written in Greek. We would like to thank Ka.Psi.Mi. publications for permission to use some of the material in those books. Michalis Veliziotis and Spiros Papakonstantinou provided excellent research assistance throughout the writing of the book and the book has benefited greatly from their input.

A large number of people, both activists and academics, contributed to the Greek books and we are grateful for the opportunity to thank them again here. For this particular book, many took the time to discuss the large number of new issues that we wanted to raise. Special thanks are due to John Milios, Heather Gibson, Andreas Kakridis, Dimosthenes Papadatos, Nikolas Sevastakis and Christos Simos. Haris Konstantatos, Elias Chronopoulos, and Andreas Xanthos were kind enough to share their valuable insights with respect to some of the social and political movements discussed in Chapter 5.

The ideas of this book have been tested over the last five years or so in countless open political meetings, discussion groups, conferences, student gatherings and other fora where literally thousands of people have expressed a remarkable interest in discussing the causes of the current crisis and the nature of left-wing alternatives or what Erik Olin Wright has labelled Real Utopias. Our book would have been very different, not to say much poorer, without the contributions and insights of those that attended such gatherings.

Finally, we owe a debt to our partners, Evi and Heather, for their forbearance once again throughout both the gatherings and the writing of the book. It is to them that we dedicate this book. We would also like to thank Christina Tsochatzi for invaluable help in preparing the book for publication

Christos Laskos and Euclid Tsakalotos

Introduction:
The Greek Crisis in Context

This book makes four interrelated arguments about the nature of the Greek crisis, and how it relates to the world economic crisis and especially to that of the Eurozone. Our major contention is that Greece is far from being a special case. The severity of the Greek crisis is not, as is often asserted, the result of either underdevelopment, or the failure to promote neoliberal structural reforms. On the contrary, the Greek crisis represents a crisis of a particular neoliberal political settlement. It follows that one needs to understand not only the underlying causes of the world economic crisis that broke out in 2008, but also why the economic and financial architecture of the Eurozone was inadequate to meet the challenges set by such a crisis. The problematic nature of that architecture also needs to be addressed in terms of its neoliberal foundations – the alternative conceptualization that the root cause lies in an incomplete fruition of the neoliberal modernizing drive within the Eurozone as a whole lacks even the superficial appeal of the similar argument made for Greece.

The policies of austerity which, at least after the initial period of the crisis, came to dominate, and not only within the Eurozone, point to a hardening of the neoliberal political and social order. The space for responding to demands and aspirations from below seems to have drastically narrowed even compared to the period of neoliberal hegemony before the crisis. Such a hardening may suggest either that elites have isolated themselves from the realities of the lived experiences of the many or, alternatively, that they lack the confidence to incorporate ideas and solutions stemming from outside their narrow circle – Ayn Rand and Friedrich Hayek may have been useful to elites in the dark days of the social-democratic consensus, but they are unlikely to provide much of a road map in the conditions of the present crisis. This lack of plasticity suggests that the final resolution to the crisis is unlikely to entail a return to either the neoliberalism of the pre-2008 period or the earlier social-democratic Keynesian consensus. We need to recall that there was no return to the *status quo ante* in the two previous major crises of capitalism in the 1930s and 1970s. Thus, we might be moving either in the direction of a far more authoritarian capitalist settlement, or to a long period of transcendence of some of the essential features of capitalism. The interest of the Greek case lies in the fact that the very acuteness of the crisis has brought to the fore both potentialities.

THE ARGUMENT STATED

For the purposes of exposition these arguments can be summarily presented in the form of four theses.

Thesis 1: Non-Exceptionality

The dominant narrative, and not only within Greece, suggests that Greece is in many ways an exceptional case with respect to the events that unfolded after 2008. This narrative is made up of three distinct, but interrelated, threads. Firstly, even liberal critics of European austerity policies, such as Paul Krugman or Martin Wolf, suggest that fiscal irresponsibility is the root cause of Greece's economic woes. Whereas many other European economies, such as Spain and Ireland, did not exhibit any evident fiscal looseness on the eve of the crisis, this cannot be said of Greece, where the financial crisis can be seen as the *result* of a fiscal crisis and not the cause.

Secondly, the cause of fiscal irresponsibility is linked to fundamental flaws within Greece's long-standing clientelistic political system. In particular, it is suggested that a nexus of political parties, the state, and sectional interests have led to a political settlement that can only be kept afloat by ever-increasing deficits and debt. Corollaries of this argument suggest that Greece is a prime example of a society that 'consumes more than it produces', or that is far more interested in 'distributing the pie rather than increasing its size'.

Thirdly, both the fiscal crisis and the skewed political arrangements are to be understood in terms of Greece's failure to develop and modernize. In particular, it is argued, Greece was more or less untouched by those 'structural' (code for neoliberal) reforms that dominated the agenda in the rest of the world from the 1980s onwards. A bloated and inefficient state, an inflexible labour market, and product markets ridden with regulations and discriminatory practices resulted in an uncompetitive economy as evidenced in large current account deficits and increasing net foreign debt. In short, by 2010, when the Greek crisis exploded onto the world scene, the chickens had truly come home to roost.

It is difficult to exaggerate the importance of this narrative, not least in terms of legitimizing the policies of austerity, which were inaugurated in 2010 when Greece was forced to agree the first adjustment programme with its official creditors. What we have, in effect, is a version of Angela Merkel's Calvinist fable, in which the unrighteous need to be punished for their past failings – both for their own good and 'pour encourager les autres'. Within Greece itself, the crudest version of this theme was promoted by Theodoros Pangalos, a long-standing and prominent politician with PASOK (Greece's socialist party) who had served in nearly every centre-left administration since 1981, whether populist or modernizing, and his memorable phrase 'we all had our snouts in the trough'.[1] Pangalos sought to implicate wide sections of the population that had benefited, even if in some cases in rather minor ways, from clientelistic politics. But crudeness does not rule out effectiveness. This exercise in creating collective guilt, implicating the whole 'culture' of the population, was a continuous and powerful refrain on the part of those intellectuals within the dominant narrative who backed the policies with which the elites proposed to address Greece's longstanding economic, political and cultural shortcomings in the age of crisis.

Our own narrative could hardly be more different. We will argue that Greece was, by 2008, well on the way to establishing a neoliberal economic order and a corresponding form of political governance. To be sure, the Greek economy and its polity had various special features, but in no way do these make the case for exceptionalism. The Greek neoliberal settlement shares many of the characteristics of similar experiments elsewhere as well as many of the failings of such experiments. In other words, the Greek crisis is better understood as a crisis of a particular neoliberal settlement rather than in terms of a failure to accept and implement the main tenets of neoliberalism.

It is not that Greece was not ridden by clientelistic politics. On the contrary, this phenomenon was an active ingredient in the legitimization of elite priorities in the whole of the post-1974 period.[2] Elsewhere, the welfare state (during the period of social democracy) and the financial system (during the period of neoliberalism) can be seen as functional equivalents promoting the overall legitimacy of the system.[3] Part of the explanation for the perseverance of the crisis (as we shall argue in Chapter 3) has to do with the fact that these mechanisms of legitimization (welfare state-loans-clientelism), all of which are attempts to spread the gains of capitalism to wider sections of the population, have come to be seen as unviable; at least in their present forms.

In the Greek case, modernizing strategies were drafted onto existing clientelistic arrangements rather than replacing them. This contention could, of course, be accepted by the dominant narrative and blamed for the eventual failure of the whole exercise. However, in a context lacking either a developed welfare state or a mature financial system, what would have replaced the legitimizing contribution of clientelism if modernization had entailed a more radical break with the clientelistic tradition? It is not clear that modernizers ever seriously addressed this issue. It could be argued that a more genuine neoliberal solution would have provided its own legitimization through results, growth, employment and rising wages. But this sanguine expectation is not borne out by the experience of more 'liberal' economies elsewhere.

We shall argue that the critique of populism of the dominant narrative, which often expresses dissatisfaction with the whole culture, is both superficial and misplaced. For in fact, both clientelism and neoliberal modernization promote individualism and undercut cooperation and solidarity. The dominant narrative not only legitimizes the inequalities and new forms of discrimination associated with all neoliberal experiments, but it also patronizingly treats peoples' yearning for a sense of belonging, for a narrative continuity for their own presence, as part of a traditional form of protest which merely blocks the necessary reforms.

Our first thesis of non-exceptionality has the added advantage of simplicity, as counselled by Ockham's razor: when so many seemingly different economies in the Eurozone are in crisis at the same time, parsimonious explanations surely entail the search for common underlying causes. Chapters 1 and 2 explore the alternative narrative we are suggesting and provide considerable evidence against the case for treating Greece as an exceptional case. We also provide empirical evidence that challenges some of the accepted 'truths' of the dominant narrative, whether this has to do with the supposedly poor performance of the Greek economy, the size of the public sector, or the argument that Greece *as a whole* consumed more than it produced. We will contend that on the eve of the crisis in 2008 Greece shared many of the characteristics, both strengths and weaknesses, evidenced in other neoliberal economies.

Thesis 2: A Crisis of Neoliberalism and Capitalism

At one level the world crisis is a crisis of neoliberalism. It is no accident that the crisis began in the more liberal economies – those that had taken the tenets of neoliberalism most seriously – and not 'statist' France or, for that matter, Greece. The proximate causes of the crisis – the financial system, social inequalities and macroeconomic imbalances – are all integrally connected to the neoliberal settlement. But precisely because that settlement was itself a response to the previous crisis of the 1970s, we are entitled to consider 2008 as a major crisis of capitalism itself. In Chapter 3 we give an account of both the world crisis and that of the Eurozone. Here we can briefly introduce some of the essential features of the crisis.

Capitalist crises are not monocausal. David Harvey (2010) has described how, over such a long period of time, it is unlikely to be the case that one could elevate one cause of the crisis above all others. In his account, a crisis of overaccumulation that became evident in the 1960s and came to fruition in the 1970s led to the neoliberal response in the 1980s. The attempt to squeeze wages and reorder labour relations, in order to restore profits, led to a latent underconsumption crisis. This in turn was, in the more liberal economies at least, staved off by cheap loans to wider sections of the population; the financial sector taking up some of the roles previously apportioned to the welfare state (in Greece, as we saw above, a different solution was readily at hand). This in turn led to the financial crisis. One need not accept all the nuts and bolts of Harvey's schema. But his way of looking at things has considerable advantages. It diverts us from the holy grail of finding the *one* underlying cause of the crisis, while at the same time leaving plenty of room for variations on the main theme: one needs to look at the long term and be open to the possibility that the nature of a crisis can change through time and across space. Harvey's approach also allows us to see why capitalist crises are often rather intractable affairs – precisely because they are not monocausal, solving one aspect of the crisis can lead to the underlying problem appearing again in a different guise.

Capitalist crises are to be explained endogenously. This would hardly need to be stated if it was not for the fact that so much of orthodox thinking, especially within economics, adopts the opposite standpoint. The dominant view appears to be that the market economy is a stable entity, and that most problems arise from the exogenous interventions of the state and/or sectionalist interests. The link to the dominant narrative on the Greek case could hardly be stronger. But the very fact that the crisis started after two decades of neoliberalism, and in the more liberal economies to boot, has severely strained credulity with respect to exogenous conceptualizations.

Capitalist crises have many moments. In short, the economic aspects of the crisis may be critical, but they constitute one 'moment' amongst others (Hall and Massey, 2010). The *political moment* is itself multidimensional. Thus, how various elites in different economies sought to plough back the gains of labour of the first two decades after World War II is subject to important variation. Furthermore, politics intermediates between capitalist crises and their resolution. In Chapter 3 we will be stressing the hollowing out of democracy that was such a hallmark of neoliberal governance. The increase in private power as a result of both privatization and deregulation – the reliance on 'independent' central banks and other regulatory authorities, the marginalization of deliberative bodies and the attacks on trade unions – are only some of the tendencies behind this retreat of democracy. Such a retreat is also relevant to the *social moment*.

The possible incompatibility between capitalism and full employment had already been indicated by Kalecki in 1943. The polish Marxist economist had argued that only new and democratic institutions, to mediate the competing class claims of capital and labour, could transcend this incompatibility. But such institutions as were promoted in the 'golden age' of capitalism were targeted by the forces of neoliberalism after 1980. One could almost go so far as saying that their destruction constituted neoliberalism's *raison d'être*. The dramatic rise in social inequality that developed in the more liberal economies, and the problems of legitimization that appeared in most economies where the neoliberal experiment took root, also needs to be seen in this light.

The *ideological moment* is also multidimensional, but an important dimension is the increasingly widespread disenchantment with the individualist creed. The disgust with bonuses in the financial sector and the prominence of so many episodes of corruption connected with private greed are only two aspects of this phenomenon. Equally important are: the social dislocation that has resulted from neoliberal policies; the feeling of not belonging to any wider collectivity that is a widespread reaction among those losing out due to market competition; the belief that ordinary people cannot control those decisions that have a significant bearing on their lives. All these have led to what John O'Neill (1998) calls a loss of 'narrative continuity', an essential element in a proper understanding of what is entailed by autonomy: many sections of society cannot make much sense of their role in society, how they relate to others, and how they relate to the wider environment.

Thesis 3: The Lack of Plasticity in the Post-2008 Political Order

The regulation of the financial system, the bonuses of financial managers and by implication the issue of inequality, the international economic order and the macroeconomic imbalances that had become such an ingrained component of that order, and the effects of possessive individualism on social cohesion, were all put onto the agenda of elite discussions in the early period after the crisis. But after the initial shock, and some expansionary interventions – especially those deemed necessary for saving the banking system – such items gradually took a back seat. Elites drew a long breath, and convinced themselves that soon there would be a relatively smooth return to the *status quo ante*. Even when it became clear that the crisis was unlikely to be a temporary blip, the policy agenda remained remarkably narrow. Most significantly, the loaded term 'reform' kept its mutated meaning: measures that extend the market's scope and increase the exposure of working people to competition and the vagaries of the market. The contrast with its meaning in the earlier period of the social-democratic consensus could hardly be more stark.

More remarkable still was the seeming inability of the elites to incorporate even minor appeals and proposals stemming from the victims of both the crisis and the subsequent policies of austerity. The unemployed, those in danger of losing their homes because of outstanding mortgage payments, and pensioners all faced a brick wall. Demonstrations, strikes and the phenomenon of the 'indignados' in the town squares, especially in Southern Europe, had little impact on governments and policymakers, thereby accentuating the social, political and ideological moments of the crisis. Such inflexibility led to spasmodic responses to the crisis that were unable to deal with recession and stagnation, let alone the deeper issues behind the crisis.

The $64 million question in this context is: why did the crisis of 2008 not present itself as an opportunity for social democracy to reassess its commitment to neoliberalism? After all, it could have argued that in the previous period it had been compelled, given the balance of forces, to accommodate the rise of neoliberalism while at the same time moderating the full effect of the approach.

It could have sought a new hegemonic role with an agenda around the regulation of the banks, a dose of Keynesian expansion, and a partial decommodification of social goods – for instance in the areas of health and education.

One hypothesis is that social democrats were in what has been termed 'cognitive locking' (Blyth, 2002): after so many years of neoliberal hegemony they were unable to step out of the groove and see the world from a different perspective. At the same time neoliberals of all stripes could be considered hostage to their own rhetoric. For instance, the financial and economic architecture of the Eurozone was built on the premise that economic crises would never materialize in the new globalized liberal economic order, thereby negating the need for economic tools should these premises prove false.

But there may be deeper forces at work here. An alternative hypothesis may be that the revival of capitalism under neoliberalism, such as it was, was based on the rise of finance and the expansion of capital into health and education. In that sense, a new social-democratic agenda could be incompatible with the profitability requirements of capitalism, at least at the present conjuncture. Interestingly, such a hypothesis was indirectly given credence by Larry Summers with his contribution to the *Financial Times* (8 January 2012) series on 'capitalism in crisis'. In an article, with the significant title 'Current woes call for smart reinvention not destruction', Summers claims the crisis has deeper, in essence technological, causes. Demand in advanced capitalist economies has been shifting from food, to clothing and household appliances, and more recently to health and education. But 'the difficulty is that in many of these areas the *traditional* case for market capitalism is weaker' (emphasis added). This could have indicated as a solution a new social-democratic rebalancing in favour of public social services. But the slant of the article, as indicated by the title, is in a rather different direction: the growth of the public sector needs to be checked, presumably because capital needs to go forward into all areas of social life if it is to survive.

At a more political level, other considerations may be playing their role. Capital has not forgotten the experience of two decades of social democracy after the war. This ended in the late 1960s and the early 1970s with an emboldened working class in many countries demanding ever increasing wages and improved labour relations, as well as experimenting, depending on the national context, in factory occupations, wage earner funds, and other innovations which challenge the power of capital. It is not an experience that capital would readily want to repeat. In short, capital may have an interest in deregulation even if this entails some sacrifice in overall economic performance (Wright, 2004). In the early years after 2008, the lack of plasticity may thus be best explained by the class instinct of capital: lacking an overall strategy for the banks or the crisis of legitimacy, austerity commended itself on the grounds of weakening labour, the better to be able to impose some kind of institutional solution at some later date, but on capital's terms. In Chapter 4 we address the policies of austerity that stem from this lack of plasticity, and in Chapter 5 we give an account of the many forms of opposition that sprung up as a consequence.

Thesis 4: No Turning Back

The above suggests that we are unlikely to return to the period of neoliberalism as experienced in the period before 2008. A settlement under the even greater hegemony of neoliberalism is likely to end up as neoliberalism transformed. We have some indication of what this may entail in Angela Merkel's vision of a federal Europe, with fiscal conservatism entrenched in a new constitution, Southern Europe as a vast reservoir of cheap labour and 'flexible' labour markets, and competition from the East acting as a permanent ceiling on any demand for social improvements.

But we have also indicated that there may be very significant obstacles to a return to the social-democratic consensus. The Keynesian contention that once we have full employment 'the classical case holds' has not stood the test of recent economic history. Thus a more liberalized financial system did not ensure that finance went to areas where it was most needed – the bubbles in real estate, stock markets and new financial instruments, to preserve the Orwellian euphemism, are evidence enough. Furthermore what growth that there was left much to be desired: the deskilling of large sections of the population, the quality of available jobs, the rise of precarious labour, the neglect (to put it no stronger) of the environment, and the decline of free time are only some of the wider qualitative issues that are not well served by capitalism, even when the issue of demand has been solved.

The no-turning-back thesis suggests that the most likely resolution to the crisis will be either in the direction of a far more authoritarian capitalism or moves to transcend capitalism in some important dimensions. In the light of this, the search for alternatives becomes a pressing issue that is taken up in Chapter 6. The Greek experience is highly revealing for both trajectories. Since 2012, Greece has experienced what moving in a more authoritarian direction entails. It has been a guinea pig, exploring what peoples in other economies could conceivably be willing to put up with. Can a capitalist economy survive without a modern welfare state, without access to finance for those on lower and middle incomes, or without whatever safety valve can be provided by clientelistic politics? Can the Eurozone resolve the issue of the South without fiscal transfers and other means to address regional divergences? Is the authoritarian federal vision capable of answering the problem of legitimacy? Developments in Greece have a bearing on these, and other, important questions. Similarly, the scale of the resistance in Greece to the policies of austerity has put a very different exit strategy from the crisis on the agenda. From our perspective that is where the main interest of the Greek case lies.

METHODOLOGICAL COMMITMENTS

Hollande's position is both strong and weak. There is the inherent strength of being a newly elected president of France. But he oversees a sclerotic economy that every month is forfeiting its competitiveness and widening the performance gap with Germany following years of failure by all French leaders to reform. If he can tackle these taboos and turn that record around, he will be in a much stronger position vis-à-vis Berlin

But his appeal and his warning demonstrate he is not backing down in the argument with Germany about how to make Europe fit for the future. He is also looking for a new deal with Merkel. Without that compromise, Europe's worst ever crisis will get worse yet.

This extract comes from Ian Traynor, the *Guardian*'s European editor, and was posted on its excellent Eurozone crisis blog (17 October 2012) on the eve of yet another European Council meeting to sort out the Eurozone crisis. It is interesting because Traynor is far from being an unthinking neoliberal and clearly, as the extract demonstrates, supported a change in agenda. And yet the extract is indicative of the kind of cognitive locking already mentioned. Notice first how the meaning of reform is taken as given, as if there is no issue concerning its direction. Notice further that all French leaders are found wanting with respect to their reforming zeal, as if France has not been on a neoliberal trajectory since Mitterrand's

1983 abandonment of the Common Programme of the Left, and as if the Socialist Party could not claim that most privatizations had been undertaken under its administrations. All this suggests a rather greater convergence, on the part of the centre-left and centre-right in France, in the direction of neoliberal reform than implied by Traynor.

Competitiveness is presented as an equally unproblematic concept with the 'necessary' adjustments – in terms of wage reductions, more flexible labour markets, and smaller firing and hiring costs – hardly needing to be spelt out. This allows little room for, say, the idea that low wages in Germany are part of the problem in the Eurozone, which could be addressed through pressure on the surplus-'competitive' economies to expand and not just the deficit-'uncompetitive' economies to contract. Behind all this lies a hardly disguised version of modernization where all economies need to converge on the most advanced, and of course more liberal, economy. The implicit compromise is always the US. With this in mind, the reference to 'taboo' can also be easily deconstructed: we all know the nature of the problem, and it is only sectionalist and special interests that prevents us from dealing with it. Finally, the major fault line is presented as being between nation states. This leaves little scope for any understanding, which suggests, alternatively, that working people in the South and North have a common interest in challenging capital and political elites in both North *and* South.

Our methodological commitments in this book challenge all these elements of cognitive locking – an essential prerequisite, we feel, for exploring a different exit from the crisis.

Ideas Matter

In recent years there has been a significant reconsideration of the role of economic ideas, and in particular their relationship to both interests and institutions. As Mark Blyth (2002) has argued, ideas are particularly important in moments of uncertainty when established institutions do not seem to be working. Such moments, often associated with large or small crises of capitalism (in the interwar period, in the 1970s, and of course now), need to be interpreted by the various economic and political actors. For instance, the ideas that have been crucial to neoliberalism (monetarism, public choice and so on) became dominant exactly because they were able to give an interpretation to the decline of the 'golden age' of capitalism: the main problem in most economies is inflation rather than unemployment, the state has the tendency to strangle private initiative, and the welfare state weakens the incentives that workers face in the labour market. Such interpretations have the ability to become a materialist force that allows people to understand reality, including the basic causal relationships that operate within the economy – for example, between government deficits and inflation.

By doing this they help people clarify where their interests lie. Thus, in the late 1970s monetarist ideas were instrumental in convincing many capitalists that their interests no longer rested with consensual arrangements with labour and the corporatist institutions that had underpinned such arrangements in the post-war period. A little later, under the influence of similar ideas, important sections of the working class shifted to the right – the Reagan Democrats constituting the paradigmatic case. Of course, such a shift reflected materialist interests, in that many skilled workers were facing higher taxes with lesser benefits (Blackburn, 1999). But this was not seen by them as a result of the attempt by the dominant classes to restore their economic and political power. On the whole they saw their deteriorating economic circumstances through the lenses of neoliberal ideas – large state, subsidies to benefit scroungers, and so on. So, as Blyth concludes, ideas are also crucial to the formation of social coalitions and the institutions and policies that such coalitions promote.

What Finlayson (2010: 22–3) calls 'naming the crisis' is likely to be as crucial in the present conjuncture. But such naming must be socially grounded. Politics is not just about grand narratives, and part of the present problems of social democracy can be understood from this perspective. A narrative (an interpretation of the crisis) that puts the blame on social democracy's traditional social base, and which offers no solution in terms of an agenda on jobs, wages and pensions, is unlikely to appeal to that base. A similar case will be made concerning the dominant narrative in Greece. The argument of this book is that for the first time in many generations the Left has a convincing interpretation of the present crisis, and that this can become a materialist force breaking old social alliances and forming new ones in favour of a strategy that begins the transcendence of capitalism itself.

The Dead End of Modernization

Modernisation is the ideology of the never-ending present. The whole past belongs to 'traditional society', and modernisation is a technical means for breaking with the past without creating a future. All is now; restless, visionless, faithless: human society diminished to a passing technique. No confrontation of power, values or interests, no choice between competing priorities is envisaged or encouraged. It is a technocratic model of society, conflict-free and politically-neutral, dissolving genuine social conflicts in abstractions of 'the scientific revolution', 'consensus', 'productivity'. (S. Hall, E.P. Thompson and R. Williams, 1968, *May Day Manifesto*)

It is remarkable how strongly this extract, from over 40 years ago, still resonates. While the modernization approach has been subject to remorseless criticism at the level of academic discourse, it still operates as a strong attractive force at the level of politics. In Greece one could go so far as to say that it has been the dominant ideology from more or less the beginning of the republic in the first half of the nineteenth century. Like most ideologies it sees itself as beleaguered in a sea of opposition, foot-dragging, and sectionalist interests. Suffice it to say here we will be arguing that it constitutes the disease that has mistaken itself for the cure. Modernization offers little help in the issues that have arisen in the present crisis.

Beyond Economism

We have already indicated that we see the crisis as one of many moments. For instance, fiscal deficits and debt cannot be taken as an exogenous independent variable of the crisis. On the contrary, such fiscal imbalances are an indication of deeper political and social problems which are themselves tied to the issue of legitimization. But the issue is much more serious than this. Polanyi's (1957 [1944]) critique of the economistic fallacy, namely that the *raison d'être* of all action and all institutions is basically economic in nature, has lost none of its moral and analytical force. Any working economy draws strength, for instance to promote trust and cooperation, from institutions that were not created for this purpose (Streeck, 1997). Our interdependence and reliance on a common framework is often the first victim of economism, especially when it is part of an individualistic and pro-market ideology. Moreover, in all versions of modernization, including leftist ones (as we shall see), the qualitative aspects of development tend to get marginalized.

Democracy and the Economy

The belief that economics is like engineering, and that one model fits all, has a corrosive effect not only on economies but the quality of democracy in western societies.[4] The technocratic-rationalist model is a close cousin of both modernization and economism. Common to all three is the cloak of objectivity, which hides value-laden choices in terms of both goals and means. Thus, even the criteria of success become value-laden, so that countries are ranked with respect to competitiveness in terms of flexibility of labour markets, as if there is widespread agreement that low wages are the key to competitiveness; or with respect to corruption in terms of the perceptions of businessmen on public sector corruption while keeping private sector corruption out of sight.

A corollary of the technocratic-rationalist model is the critique of 'populism'. As the Eurozone crisis developed, politicians and officials, especially those concerned with the slowness of the response, would argue that unless important steps were taken the forces of populism would continue to strengthen. In Greece itself the critique of populism was an integral component of the dominant narrative. The idea that those protesting against austerity could actually be right, that new ideas and solutions could come from social movements, that a narrative for a different Europe needs the idea of a European people, and thus that important changes come from initiatives from below and not elite adjustments, is completely missing from such a narrative. The link between democracy and the economy should be at the core of the Left's response to the current crisis.

The Nation and the Demos

Our methodological commitments, finally, need to address the issue of the nation state as an analytical category, and in particular the concept of national competitiveness. It is part of the rules of the game of globalization that its basic tenets are beyond dispute. These rules supposedly stem from technological factors too powerful for any nation state to confront; or they derive from the very nature of modernity, in which it is argued that it is the individual that cannot be held back by traditional commitments or identities. Under these determinants the nation state does not lose its role, but that role changes in significant ways. In particular, the nation state becomes a key actor in the competitive rat race, in ensuring the survival of its citizens in the new global economic order. Nation states that do not play by the book can expect the harsh judgment of financial markets and all that entails. Should, from time to time, the global rules need changing, then this is a task for negotiation and bargaining between nation states, as can be seen from the extract from Ian Traynor above.

Between the global rules and the nation state, the demos, let alone class, disappear from sight. It is hardly a conceptualization that can commend itself to anyone interested in looking for alternatives in the present crisis.

We have ended with a set of methodological commitments in part because modernization, the technocratic spirit, economism and an ethnocentric approach to economic policy are not foreign to many left-wing approaches. In Chapter 6 we will have the opportunity to explore these issues more fully as we examine disagreements within the Greek Left on the appropriate response to the crisis. There we will offer a critique of left-wing responses to the previous crisis, and suggest that this time round we need a Left which is more democratic, more participatory, and more aware that supranational problems need supranational responses.

1
Neoliberalism as Modernization

The Greek people have never been entirely comfortable with either modernity or their place in the world. Wars, occupation, civil wars, massive waves of both emigration and immigration, and a plethora of dictatorial or authoritarian regimes hardly provided fertile ground for self-confidence. They have had their moments of course; most recently with their participation in the euro area in 2001, and, albeit in a more Pyrrhic mode, their organization of a successful Olympic Games in 2004. But the impression always lingered that any success would prove purely temporary; that underneath there lurked fundamental flaws related to incomplete modernization and, in particular, the lack of a proper state. Not surprisingly the feeling that sooner or later 'they would be found out' surfaced with a vengeance when the Greek crisis broke out in earnest in the first months of 2010. The dominant narrative of the crisis, already sketched out in the Introduction of this book, sought to transform this feeling into both an interpretation of what had gone wrong and a recipe for how to set Greece, at last, on an irreversible path of modernization.

According to this dominant narrative, at stake were not alternative visions for the economy and society for the post-neoliberal era: no clash of values, merely one between backward- and forward-looking cultures. For, so the argument went, Greece constituted the great exception among EU member states (Ioakeimides, 2011). It had never experienced neoliberalism; appeals to the latter no more than a delaying tactic from those seeking to obstruct all change. Thus, the Greek crisis was more related to the accumulation of internal problems than a consequence of the world economic crisis of neoliberal capitalism that broke out in 2008. The appropriate response lay, therefore, in the implementation of those modernizing reforms that would have been necessary irrespective of the crisis.

In the following chapters we seek to challenge this idea that Greece's woes stem from an incomplete modernization, and attempt to situate the Greek crisis firmly within the evolving crisis of the Eurozone. For the moment we turn to making the case that from the mid-1990s onwards Greek elites pursued, with some success, a reform programme with impeccable neoliberal credentials.

STYMIED MODERNIZATION AND THE CLASH OF CULTURES

Writing in 1994, the political scientist Nikiforos Diamandouros[5] addressed Greece's longstanding internal problems in terms of a clash between two cultures, which, he contended, had been going strong ever since the creation of the Greek Republic in the late 1820s. His problematic is firmly within the modernization approach that was once so influential, particularly in the US, in both political and economic science. The basic idea is that most societies will eventually converge onto the political, economic and social institutions of the advanced capitalist countries. The attractiveness of these institutions is rarely discussed,[6] nor is much thought given to the shifting trajectory of the goal, as if approaching Johnson's 'Great Society' constitutes a similar exercise to approaching the neoconservative vision of Bush the Younger. Given this relative indifference to ends, the analysis is more concerned with examining the obstacles to modernization,[7] for it is acknowledged that there are costs involved in this process of catch-up which are 'unavoidable (and, according to many, necessary)' (Diamandouros, 1994: 113).

In the Greek case, Diamandouros contends that those forces that have most to lose have attached themselves to a culture that has had a particular take on economics, politics and international affairs: inward-looking,[8] suspicious of foreigners, statist, anti-market, and pro-redistribution. Moreover, this 'underdog' culture has been able to offer powerful resistance to the outward-looking and pro-market 'reform' culture, which has sought to modernize Greece. The clash of cultures has delayed the modernization of both society and the economy, or, at best, led to reforms that have been half-hearted and incomplete.[9]

From this, and similar perspectives that prevail within the dominant narrative, Greek history since the metapolitefsi – the term given to the period after the fall of the seven-year junta – can be written in terms of turns not taken, of opportunities missed. After the restoration of democracy in 1974 there were governments of the centre-right until 1981, with Konstantinos Karamanlis, the founder of the New Democracy Party, as prime minister until 1980. The 1980s were dominated by the centre-left administrations (1981–89) of PASOK led by Andreas Papandreou. In the dominant narrative these two prominent, not to say domineering, personalities of the post-1974 period get a rather mixed assessment.

Karamanlis is credited primarily with negotiating Greece's successful accession to the EU in 1981, a critical moment since Greece's ever closer integration within Europe is considered a critical component of any serious strategy of modernization; external pressure making up for domestic recalcitrance. His partial accommodation of the unions, especially those in the public sector, as well as of an increasingly confident student and wider education movement, is seen in more equivocal terms. On the one hand, the emphasis on social and democratic rights, as well as some nationalization in the banking and productive sectors, are accepted as unavoidable correctives in order to redress the social and political injustices that had evolved in the aftermath of Greece's civil war in the late 1940s and the period of dictatorship (1967–74). On the other hand, the failure to seriously engage with Greece's economic problems, and in particular with respect to its overprotected productive structure, as well as a reticence to touch Greece's statist legacy, are seen in terms of sowing the seeds of future economic disaster.

This account is somewhat partial. For instance, in seeking to make a case for Greek exceptionalism, almost from the year dot, it passes too lightly over the wider zeitgeist of the period. For all the talk in Greece at the time of 'social mania' (i.e. extreme social sensitivities), it takes some effort to remember now that this direction was not out of line with developments elsewhere. Even in the US, Nixon's first response to the end of the long post-war boom was in terms of price and wage controls, and in 1975 the Humphrey Hawkins Bill was introduced, which included the notion of the government as the employer of last resort.[10] Statism and suspicion of market solutions, the two great *bêtes noires* of the modernizing tendency, were not, in the 1970s at least, exclusive to the Greek underdog culture. More serious still is the fact that, as we will go on to see, this social mania hardly began to address Greece's accumulated social and democratic deficit (Dragasakis, 2012). While later contributions to the dominant narrative would bemoan the hegemony of leftist ideas in the early metapolitefsi period,[11] the persistence of social inequalities and the realities of elite power hardly justify these claims.

The dominant narrative is also equivocal with respect to the subsequent PASOK administrations of Andreas Papandreou, but with a more negative assessment overall. Thus, while some social interventions, most notably the creation of the national health service, are given a positive assessment, the initial attempted redistribution, through significant increases in wages and pensions between 1981 and 1983, is deemed as being far ahead of what the economy could bear. Not surprisingly therefore, the subsequent economic crisis in 1985 led to the first of many stabilization attempts (1985–87), the reversal of most of the gains in real wages if not pensions, and the end of PASOK's more radical phase. This signalled the abandonment of the half-hearted experiments with planning agreements, socialization of public industries, and a more interventionist industrial policy.[12]

For modernizers, who in any case exhibit little interest in social experimentation that is not sanctioned by the calls of modernity, this abandonment was merely a belated wake-up call with respect to reality. More crucial, for them, is that it did not signal a permanent shift to a coherent programme of modernization: for the stabilization programme, significantly (for the story to be told) under the leadership of Kostas Simitis at the Ministry of the National Economy, was also abandoned. What replaced it were spasmodic policy initiatives with little overall coherence or direction, primarily geared to the needs of populist politics. Untenable pre-election promises to all and sundry, state agreements with selected private sector firms, and special tax breaks for some social groups are just some of the elements in the nexus of party, state and sectionalist interests. Giannis Voulgaris, another prominent modernizing political scientist, includes both PASOK and the Left in his critique of those parties that shored up this nexus, which rested on redistribution and consumption with little interest in the culture of production, competitiveness and innovation.[13] Such an axis was enough to block reforms, thus laying the foundations for future fiscal crisis. The major losers from this arrangement were those 'outsiders' with insufficient bargaining power to extract concessions, subsidies, tax exemptions and other goodies from the state.[14] Every grand narrative needs a worthy enemy, and for modernizers, of all persuasions, populism more than fits the bill.

The dominant narrative's account is as deficient with respect to the PASOK period as it is to that of the New Democracy period. But as we shall focus on the modernizers' critique in much of what is to come, we will not seek to address the deficiencies here. Suffice it to say that we agree with Kouvelakis' conclusion (2011: 19) that 'the social foundations of the *ancien régime* remained largely in place, not only under the Conservative New Democracy Party in the second half of the 70s, but also during the long rule of PASOK after 1981'. In this light, the charge of populism levelled against both parties needs considerable reformulation if it is not to lose all analytical coherence. Populism was a real phenomenon in Greece, but in the dominant narrative its content is extended to include nearly any popular demand or aspiration, while at the same time keeping many of the real winners from the system out of focus.[15]

For the dominant narrative then, both New Democracy and PASOK exhibited common achievements and failings. On the plus side, they both contributed to the consolidation of democracy and Greece's increasing integration with Europe.[16] But the failings, with respect to economic and political modernization, dominate. In particular, they failed to reform Greece's public administration and take on the populist forces that gained most from clientelistic politics. With respect to the latter, if anything the reliance on patron–client relations, and the traditional exchange of favours through 'rousfeti', was deepened as the two political parties organized these relations through their increasingly sophisticated party machines (Mouzelis, 1980).

By the mid-1990s, however, there was a new feeling that the tide of history was turning in favour of the modernizers. Thus Diamandouros ends his book with the prediction that the reform culture was gaining ground, especially as a consequence of the process of globalization and European integration. The change of guard in the leadership of PASOK in 1996, from Andreas Papandreou to the modernizing Kostas Simitis, seemed at the time to provide ample support for such optimism. Simitis' eight-term stint as leader of PASOK, and as prime minister, was to be a crucial test both for modernizers and the reform culture.

But by 2010, the dominant modernizing narrative's assessment was far less sanguine. The 'underdog' culture was seen to have once more succeeded in obstructing the vital reforms needed for modernization. Ioakimidis (2011) contended that the origins of the Greek crisis need to be sought in cultural prototypes and that the Greek crisis 'revolves around behaviours, values, stances, opinions'. Nikos Themelis, a distinguished novelist and close political advisor to Kostas Simitis, would argue that there was a need to examine the crisis in holistic terms.[17] The only thing remaining for modernizers was to embrace the crisis as an opportunity to finally settle things in their favour. This is the story we shall take up in Chapter 4.

For the moment, an understanding of the content and direction of the modernizing exercise in Greece is critical to understanding the subsequent crisis. We shall argue that Simitis' governments had impeccable neoliberal intent, and were far more successful in outcome than is suggested by the dominant narrative.

THE NATURE OF THE NEOLIBERAL EXERCISE

To make the case we need a brief detour to examine the essence of neoliberalism itself. We need first to distinguish between neoliberalism as an ideal type, and 'actually existing' neoliberalism. For whether implemented by parties of the centre-left or the centre-right, there were always rearguard actions to soften the edges. These usually originated from the more traditional social-democratic or popular right sections of the parties involved. The lack of purity, as well as the numerous compromises and partial reversals, of the neoliberal era do not, however, negate the nature of the overall direction in the years after the victories of Margaret Thatcher and Ronald Reagan.

At the same time, the argument that Greece largely missed the neoliberal moment relies heavily on a definition of neoliberalism as marketed by its advocates: less state, more markets; entrepreneurship and the value of individualism; equality of opportunity rather than outcome. It is not a description that readily stands the test of neoliberal theorizing, let alone neoliberal practice.

Any account that does not also include some of the following four features is unwarrantedly restrictive, and clearly ideological in intent:[18]

1. Neo-liberalism elevates capital to the status of the universal class, in the sense that its interests coincide with those of society as a whole. Private sector investments and initiatives are the source of all wealth. It follows that entrepreneurs must be given the tools to do the job, whether this entails lower wages or lower corporation taxes, or access to those activities, such as health and education, previously in the public sector.[19]
2. Financial markets can be trusted to distribute resources to where they are most needed, and over-regulation can only impede such a process. They also play the central regulative role of the system. They judge firms, and whole economies, every moment of every day. Those who do not conform to neoliberal understandings of shareholder value, efficiency and competitiveness face the sell-off of their shares/bonds, decreasing their price and increasing the cost of borrowing – with everything that entails. Realism often turns out to mean no more than an acceptance of this role on behalf of firms and governments alike.

3. The enemy is not the state but a particular form of the state (Jessop, 2002). Deregulation can lead to re-regulation as long as this ensures the profits and power of private sector enterprises. Privatizations, and the outsourcing of public social services, are to be preferred even if they lead to private sector interests and large firms with little apparent comparative advantage other than acquiring public sector contracts. Large firms are rarely a threat to the system and should be encouraged to exploit economies of scale and scope. Needless to say, a neoliberal state has no problem with enlarged military and police functions.

4. The enemy can be found in those groups that seek to limit the effects of competition on labour and interfere politically in the market to redistribute income to the 'losers' of the whole process: unions, social movements and other forms of collection action.[20]

All four features are part of the story in Greece in the period before the crisis. Neoliberal modernization started in earnest after 1996 under the leadership of PASOK's new leader Kostas Simitis. There had been previously incomplete attempts: in the period 1985–87 under PASOK, and in 1991–93 with the government of New Democracy under Konstantinos Mitsotakis. By 1996, the victory of the uncharismatic Simitis in the leadership contest to replace Andreas Papandreou heralded the victory of the modernizing wing of PASOK. Simitis himself had, from the late 1980s, cut out a space for himself as the leader of those modernizing tendencies in Greece that sought an end to the tradition of clientelistic politics and inward-looking development.

This shift in PASOK also, of course, signalled a turn to the right, with new priorities and the marginalization of traditional social-democratic concerns such as the promotion of workers' participation in the economic sphere. There is nothing exceptional in this trajectory. While centre-left governments of the 1960s and early 1970s still operated within the framework of trade union advance, Keynesian macroeconomics and the welfare state, from the 1980s onwards leaders such as Hawke, Blair and Schröder began to embrace neoliberalism (Riley, 2012). The failure of more leftist experiments, such as the *Alternative Economic Strategy* in the UK in the 1970s and the *Common Programme of the Left* in France in the early 1980s, clearly played a role in this shift. The result was not only the loss of hegemony for left-wing approaches, but that the Left as a whole barely influenced the process of globalization and European integration after the mid-1980s.

Perhaps the last time that the accommodation of the Left to the ideas of the Right was in any serious doubt was in the late 1990s, when economic conditions, financial crises and the stalling of the European integration process provided some food for thought for a number of newly elected centre-left governments. This led to a debate about the extent to which the then orthodoxy needed to be challenged. While there were clearly differences between politicians such as Lafontaine and Jospin on the one hand, and Blair and Schröder on the other, the debate centred on a number of issues: the extent to which centre-left governments should treat the existing monetary and financial framework more flexibly; whether Europe needed an additional 'economic pole' to provide more active and coordinated policies to reduce unemployment; and the role of the EU in the world economy in providing exchange rate stability through some kind of target zone system and financial stability by challenging the power of financial markets (Dyson, 1999).[21] But nothing ever came from this last window of opportunity.

PASOK under Kostas Simitis hardly murmured a note of dissent from the European centre-left relocation within the political space of neoliberalism throughout the eight years of his premiership. Its self-understanding as a pro-European party did not incorporate any vision, let alone intervention, with respect to the evolving nature of the European exercise: the details of, say, monetary union, or European employment policy, were merely seen as the way that 'proper' economies sought to modernize and integrate. There was, moreover, little concern about the democratic deficit of the EU, let alone a desire to contribute to the creation of a European public space. If there was ever any inclination to push for a Europe that could provide space for democratic and social experimentation this was rarely articulated in public. As with Andreas Papandreou, Simitis' stance towards the EU was largely instrumental. Europe was a powerful ally in carrying out preconceived reforms and marginalizing opposition to those reforms. What this really entailed was not a European ideal, but a national strategy within Europe. It was a form of provincialism that was to become, with fatal consequences, a dominant mode of thought in the post-crisis era.

If in the countries of advanced capitalism the target of much neoliberal thinking and practice was the old social-democratic state, and the social consensus that underpinned it, things were rather different in a Southern Europe that had never really gone through the era of the social-democratic consensus. Greece, Portugal and Spain have been marked by their authoritarian pasts, the ideological and institutional power of conservative forces, and by very deep social inequalities (Navarro, 2011; Streeck, 2012). In the words of Kouvelakis (2011: 19–20):

> the devastating defeat of the left in Greece in the Civil War meant that post-war Greece possessed nothing comparable to the social compromise forged elsewhere in Europe in the 50s and 60s: there was no welfare state, no social-democratic party; wage-levels continued to be miserably low and work place regimes were very repressive.

As we have seen the metapolitefsi period was, at best, a very partial response to this heritage.

This is an important point because it suggests that from the beginning the modernizers misidentified the nature of the target. Promoting some of the key features of neoliberalism, in a society already ridden with unacceptable levels of inequality, was to lead not just to an accentuation of social problems, but also to a crisis of a political system seemingly unable to respond to the needs of ever wider sections of the population.

For it is important to stress that all advanced capitalist societies, since World War II at least, have had mechanisms to spread the goods of capitalism to wider sections of the population. Most have experimented with the welfare state and the more liberal ones eventually turned to the financial system and a form of 'privatized keynesianism' (Crouch, 2011). But both these attempts to reconcile capitalism with democracy have been put under severe strain by the present crisis and that of the 1970s. In an important sense the fiscal problems of advanced capitalist countries can be seen as being the result of this strain (Streeck, 2011a).

For the above reconciliation, Greece has relied less on the welfare state and the financial system and more on the long-standing practices of the clientelistic state: employment in the public sector, special privileges to certain groups of society, the closing of the eye to tax evasion, and much more besides. A system that was as inefficient as it was unjust, but one that had traditionally contributed to keeping a lid on social pressures: directly by vertically integrating sections of society, and indirectly by undercutting horizontal and class organizations which could challenge the power of elites. By the 1990s the modernizers around Simitis had decided that reform of this system was needed if Greece was to modernize and participate as an equal partner in the process of European integration. However, it was never made clear (perhaps never even conceived as a problem) what the institutions or policies needed to address the social issue, and thus provide the legitimization of the system as a whole, would be.

Central to the whole exercise was the change in the meaning of reform. Here again there was little or no divergence in PASOK from the new norms of European social democracy. Slowly, and by stealth, the old social-democratic meaning was almost entirely inverted. From defending working people from the vagaries of the market, reform now increasingly meant, at best, helping them to manage their own (including human) capital (Giddens, 1998). At worse, it merely transferred risk onto those least able to bear it. From work being a source of creativity, or at least a *'quid pro quo* for services granted by the community', it turned into a 'far starker assumption of individual responsibility for financial independence and an activity subservient to the economic and productivity goals established by market forces' (Freeden, 1999: 47). Simitis (1989) himself had staked out his ground at the centre of a modernizing pole within PASOK with his sceptical thoughts regarding corporatist solutions and all collectivities that had the power to block the needed structural reforms. His hostility to such collective interests was never to waver.

As indicated in our synopsis of some of neoliberalism's key features, the target is not primarily the state as such. Centre-left modernizers are willing to countenance the existence of market failure, in infrastructure investments or training for instance, and thus a role for state intervention. Simitis and his economic team were of the same opinion," preferably, wherever possible, through independent authorities responsible for economic policy. But there was little recognition of how much such a conceptualization, what the economist John Kay (2007) has called the 'failure of the market failure' approach, cedes to neoliberal modes of thought. The idea, in other words, that there are areas of economic and social life that are not about individual preferences, but collective and political decision-making, which need to be protected from market exposure, is one that is by now foreign to nearly the whole of the social-democratic family. Not surprisingly, therefore, the retreat from the ideas of economic democracy, at one time the flagship of the whole movement, has been almost universal.

More worrying still, this reassessment of the importance of collective political decision-making is not confined to the economic sphere; it has spread to politics itself. For the process of convergence of centre-left and centre-right parties with respect to economics has been accompanied with the rise of 'cartel parties', a complex process wherein political parties do not only begin to resemble each other, but reorganize their relationship with the state in order to be able to exploit its resources and ensure their own reproduction (Katz and Mair, 2009). In such parties the locus of decision making, together with most of the resources of the party, shifts from the party base towards the 'party in government'. At the same time we observe looser party structures that tend to blur the differences between party members and simple supporters, while at the same time marginalizing party cadres with strong connections to the organized social base of the party. With respect to the parties of the centre-left this comes with a disinclination to organize labour on class lines, since the dominant assumption is that modern capitalism has dissolved the conflictual basis of class, and other forms, of politics. The effect of all this is to negate the very possibility of a change of political agenda coming from below.

PASOK and New Democracy provide almost paradigmatic cases of the cartel party phenomenon. And as we shall see later, this development is central to understanding the series of political scandals that erupted and that rocked the political system even before the economic crisis. For the moment, we can conclude here by stating that PASOK, under Simitis, started the process in which his party would converge, particularly on economic issues, with New Democracy, and in which the meaning of reform was fundamentally altered. It was from the start a process with little democratic sensitivity. The losers from modernization could be marginalized, defeated, or even compensated, but never incorporated into a democratic dialogue over possible futures. Modernization, as we have seen, is a journey to a given end. This then sets the limits to 'governance' structures. Debate, participation and accountability can all be encouraged, as long as they rest on a shared basis of values and the discourse of the market (De Angelis, 2007: 89–95). One can adopt best practices, one can form policy networks, and one can even set up deliberative procedures. But the technocratic essence is hard to disguise: a policy community united by a common cause and guided by common values.

INSTITUTIONAL AND POLICY INTERVENTIONS

If the target of modernization differed from similar exercises in the North, its content was not especially distinct. The idea that the good intentions of the modernizers were stymied by an alliance of public sector unions and state-reliant firms, with politicians in all political parties determined to continue with business as usual, is not supported by the evidence. The record is far more mixed than is suggested by the dominant narrative. Table 1 shows some of the key reforms implemented before the crisis.

Table 1.1   Main reforms and privatizations, 1996–2010 (pre-Memorandum of Understanding)

1996	Listing of OTE (Hellenic Telecommunications Organization) on the Athens Stock Exchange
1997	Extension of civil service hiring procedures to the hiring of teachers and workers in state companies
1997	Capodistrian Law for merging of local councils
1998	Independence granted to Bank of Greece
1998	23% of Hellenic Petroleum privatized (in a first tranche)
1998	Part-time working reformed and introduced to wider public sector
1999	Establishment of Regulatory Authority for Energy
2000	Liberalization of telecommunications market
2001	Listing of OPAP (betting organization) on Athens Stock Exchange
2003–2004	Liberalization of fixed-term contracts in private and public sectors
2005	Legal framework developed for Private–Public Partnerships
2005	Law reforming organization and operation of state companies
2005	Labour reforms to reduce cost of overtime and working time
2006	Privatization of Commercial Bank (now Emporiki Bank)
2006	Listing of Hellenic Postbank on the Athens Stock Exchange
2007	Sale of 25% of OTE to Deutsche Telekom
2009	Privatization of Olympic Airways
2010	Establishment of the Hellenic Statistical Authority (EL.STAT) as an independent institution

Sources: Kazakos (2010); Kouzis, Y. (2012) 'The Institutional Path of Flexibility and Deregulation of Labour Markets in Greece (1990–2012)', available in Greek at http://www.iskra.gr (accessed May 2013); *Social Reforms* Database, Fondazione Rodolfo Debenedetti (http://www.frdb.org/language/ita/topic/archivio-dati/dataset/international-data/doc_pk/9027 – accessed May 2013); various websites of banks and other organizations.

It is not an unimpressive list, including all the main elements in any neoliberal cookbook: liberalization, deregulation, 'independent' regulatory authorities and so on. In what follows we will focus on four elements: the reduction of corporate tax rates, the programme of privatizations, the implementation of labour market reforms, and the rising prominence of the financial system.

As can be seen from Figure 1.1, from 2000 onwards the Simitis government pursued a policy of reducing corporate tax rates. This was continued by the New Democracy government after 2004,

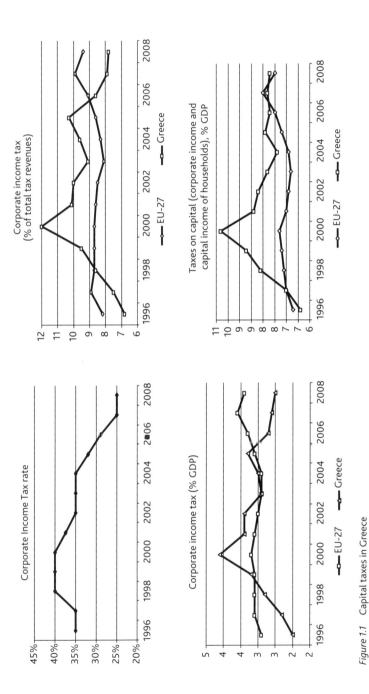

Figure 1.1 Capital taxes in Greece

Sources: OECD Tax Database; Taxation Trends in the EU 2012; DG Taxation; European Commission.

28

signposting an important convergence in the area of economic policy-making. This, unsurprisingly, although contrary to neoliberal folklore on the subject, led to a declining contribution from business to overall tax revenues, an important point that we will have occasion to return to when discussing the Greek deficit and debt crisis.

These changes represent the biggest decrease in the burden of corporate taxation since 2000 for all 27 EU member states (Deutsche Bank, 2012). So in this case, at least, the exceptionalism of Greece lies in the rigour of its allegiance to neoliberal tenets.

For all the post-crisis talk of Greece being the 'last soviet state',[23] the record with respect to privatization is revealing. As Table 1.2 shows, the Simitis period (1996–2008) was particularly important in this respect. Both in terms of the number of privatizations and the revenue gained, the Greek experience stands up very well with the experience of other countries in the Eurozone (Ioannides, 2012).

Table 1.2   Privatizations in Greece, 1991–2008

	Number	Revenue (% GDP)
1991–1993	13	1.2
1993–1996	1	0.3
1996–2000	26	5.8
2000–2004	18	3.3
2004–2008	8	4.2

Sources: Ioannides (2012); Privatization Barometer (http://www.feem.it/getpage.aspx?id=134& sez=research&padre=18&sub=75&idsub=101 – accessed May 2013).

Note: Total privatizations – PASOK 40, New Democracy 23.

The fact that it was PASOK that took the lead is also not exceptional. In France the Socialist Lionel Jospin also

pursued privatizations of state-owned enterprises with extraordinary vigor: during his five-year tenure, from 1997 to 2002, he privatized more than any of his 'conservative' predecessors, and almost more than all of his predecessors combined. France Telecom, Air France, Crédit Lyonnais, Aerospatial-Matra, Banque Hervet – just some of the names of the more than 900 companies that saw shares floated on the stock market. With roughly 31 billion Euros ($40 billion) in privatization revenues, Jospin left his 'conservative' predecessors, Prime Ministers Chirac (€13 billion in privatizations), Balladur (€17 billion) and Juppé (€9.4 billion) in the dust.[24]

A similar case can be made with respect to labour market reform, to which the soviet charge has also been made.[25] Many forms of casual and precarious labour were promoted in both the public and private sectors (Karamessini, 2008).[26] If we add to this the weakness, not to mention purposeful neglect, of the system of inspectors for labour relations, it is very difficult to make a case for inflexible labour markets being a major cause of the crisis. Indeed, a number of social movements arose before 2008, prefiguring the rise of the Left in the later austerity years, around the issues of precarious employment, especially for young people, and unemployment.

Finally, we can point to the liberalization and growing weight of the financial system as evidence of the direction of change in this period. Liberalization had begun tentatively in the late 1980s, but it was a central plank of all modernizers in the later period as well. There was the usual sanguine view that liberalization would lead to finance going to where it was most needed, rather than being allocated by the crony politics of the clientelistic system. While the latter, as we shall see, was not borne out by events, the relative weight of the financial system grew enormously, albeit from a relatively low base (see Figure 1.2). If Greece seemed to be moving from a reliance on tariffs and other forms of protection to a reliance on credit, this could hardly be counted as a source of exceptionality during these years.

Finance was central to both PASOK's and New Democracy's economic strategy after 1996. Mergers were encouraged, as was the impressive expansion of the Greek banking system throughout the Balkans and Turkey. Moreover, there was a growing symbiosis of financial and political power experienced elsewhere. Both parties, and their respective prime ministers, increasingly relied on bankers and financial analysts for policy advice. This merely prefigured the prominence of figures such as Lucas Papademos, prime minister in 2012, and Yiannis Stournaras, finance minister in the government of Samaras, after the outbreak of the crisis.

One could argue that Greek banks, unlike those in the US and the UK (not to mention those in Ireland and Spain), had not been modernized enough so as to be heavily implicated in the derivatives speculation that was such a prominent part of the crisis elsewhere. However, to a great extent the incentives to move into such business were not large since the liberalization of banking in the 1990s had

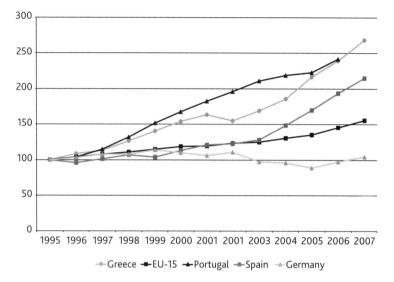

Figure 1.2 Financial intermediation – gross value added, volume index (1995 = 100)

Source: EU KLEMS Database (http://www.euklems.net/ – accessed May 2013).

Notes: Data for Portugal are only available up to 2006.

led to plenty of profitable opportunities in more traditional forms of lending: mortgages and consumer credit. Whatever the form taken by the growth of financial activity, the direction of policy towards the financial system was unmistakably neoliberal in the years before the crisis.

CONCLUSION

Were there areas of failure, or untoward delay, with respect to this neoliberal enterprise? There were, most notably in the area of pension reform and with respect to reforming the public administration,[27] to which we shall return in future chapters. But as we have already mentioned, such failures are in no way exceptional within the European neoliberal family. On the other side we need to factor in the abandonment of many of the elements of traditional social democracy and PASOK's own heritage. The idea of economic democracy, or workers' participation, was removed even from policy networks in these years. Similarly, the role of democracy in local government was hollowed out, as cash-strapped local authorities had to turn to private–public partnerships for funding; with private profitability replacing local preference as a criterion for local investment projects. The promise that state spending on education would reach 5 per cent of GDP, a perennial item in both parties' electoral manifestos, was also abandoned. Similarly, health spending, and policies towards state-run hospitals, encouraged the strong growth of the private sector.

In short, the neoliberal drive is made up of both sins of commission and of omission. Enough has been said about policy input to make the case that such a drive existed in Greece in the period before the outbreak of the crisis. What of output and outcome? Can it be said that the Greek economy remained in an underdeveloped state, which made it ill prepared to meet the crisis? Is poor economic performance the main explanatory variable for the events that followed? It is to these questions we turn to in Chapter 2. As we shall see, the case for Greek exceptionalism fairs no better in terms of output than it does in terms of input.

2
The Greek Economy and Society on the Eve of the Crisis

In one sense a crisis must always reflect past failings. But the dominant narrative is far more specific in its diagnosis with respect to the failures of the Greek case. As we have seen, the charge is that an unholy alliance of sectionalist interests, state-dependent firms and clientelistically orientated politicians blocked most of the necessary reforms, with dire consequences for entrepreneurship and those new dynamic sections of the economy that could take Greece out of its perennial state of underdevelopment. The years before 2010 were wasted, with Greeks consuming beyond their means and the political system concentrating on how the pie was to be redistributed rather than how it could be increased. Significantly, this Greek narrative was, after the outbreak of the crisis, to find a powerful echo in a European equivalent in which a thrifty and productive North permanently had to bail out a spendthrift and more leisurely South.

The narrative, in either its Greek or European version, has nuggets of truth swamped in a sea of distortion and blind spots. We have already seen that the argument that all change was blocked is not supported by the actual record of policy and institutional interventions. Here we turn our attention to outcomes, to the economic and social record. We shall show that far from being in a state of underdevelopment, the Greek economy was in many ways a success story for the period between the mid-1990s and the crisis. Moreover, this success was based on an economy that shared many of the strengths, but also the weaknesses, of the neoliberal economic order.

It is true to say that in the 'good years' – which as we shall demonstrate were far from being good for all – the opportunity was not taken to address certain important fault lines that were apparent even at the time. Structural economic problems, the persistence of social inequalities, and the deficiencies of the public administration are all part of the story. But they do not add up to make a case for Greek exceptionalism. On the contrary, they are features that will be present when we turn to analysing the Eurozone crisis as a whole in the next chapter.

THE ECONOMIC RECORD

Figure 2.1 shows that in the period between 1995 and 2008 Greek growth was consistently above the EU average, and this naturally led to a convergence of Greek GDP per capita (see Figure 2.2). Perhaps even more significant is the wider United Nations index on human development, which also captures social and educational gains, and which shows that Greece's catch-up seems to have been an uninterrupted process since the early 1980s (Figure 2.3).

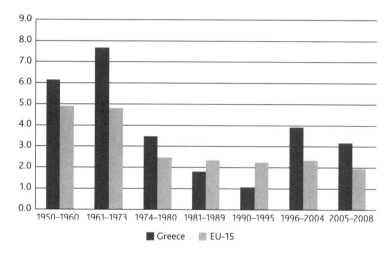

Figure 2.1 Real GDP growth

Sources: *Total Economy Database* (The Conference Board, 2011) (http://www.conference-board.org/data/economydatabase/ – accessed May 2013); authors' calculations.

Notes: Figure shows the average annual real GDP growth per country and time period. Real GDP is expressed in 1990 US$ (converted at Geary–Khamis PPPs).

Behind these impressive figures lie important success stories within the productive economy. Shipping, banking and construction dominate, as one would expect, and not only within the borders of the Greek state. For these were the years of Greek entrepreneurial expansion into Eastern Europe and Turkey, with important investments in all the countries concerned, and with outflows of FDI far exceeding inflows (Milios, 2004). To many this strategy

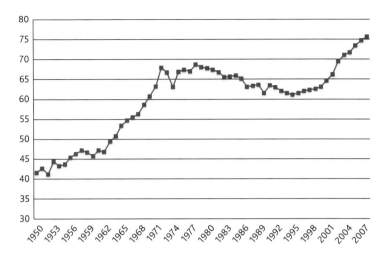

Figure 2.2   GDP per capita – Greece (EU 15 = 100)

Sources: *Total Economy Database* (The Conference Board, 2011) (http://www.conference-board.org/data/economydatabase/ – accessed May 2013); authors' calculations.

Notes: Real GDP is expressed in 1990 US$ (converted at Geary–Khamis PPPs).

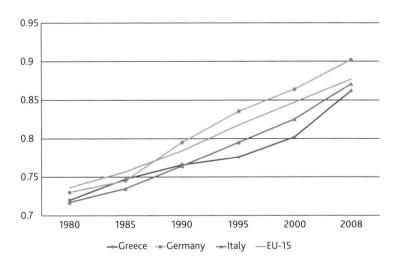

Figure 2.3   Human development index (HDI)

Source: United Nations, *Human Development Reports*, http://hdr.undp.org (accessed May 2013).

Notes: For EU 15 HDI is calculated as the average of the HDI values of the EU 15 countries.

amounted to a new national goal, replacing earlier delusions of national grandeur and expansionism.[28] Before the crisis one could walk around the streets of, say, Sofia or Bucharest, and be amazed at the banking and commercial presence – from toys to furniture and cement – of Greek companies.

Within Greece we observe newer more dynamic industrial sectors, such as electrical and optical equipment, or chemical, rubber, plastics and fuels, doing much better than more traditional sectors such as textiles, and food and beverages (see Figure 2.4).

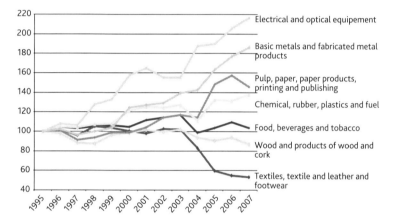

Figure 2.4   Various subsectors of manufacturing in Greece – gross value added, volume index (1995 = 100)

Source: EU KLEMS Database (http://www.euklems.net/ – accessed May 2013).

In previous work (Laskos and Tsakalotos, 2012: 37–54), we provide numerous examples of other dynamic and, from the perspective of the dominant narrative, surprising success stories. For instance, since the mid-1990s computers and related activities, as well as basic and fabricated metals, show significant growth in terms of gross value added; higher than the EU 15 average, and economies such as Spain, Portugal and Germany. Moreover, the performance is equally good in terms of productivity (gross valued added per hour worked). It is fair to say that growth in many areas started from a low base, but it is also difficult to make the case that the period is characterized by the absence of structural shifts.

Also contrary to popular perceptions, Greek economic performance was based on a solid performance with respect to investment: a real rise in fixed investment of 102.8 per cent was recorded in the period 1995–2008 (Milios and Sotiropoulos, 2011: 409). The equivalent rise in Germany was 18.8 per cent, reflecting in part, as we shall see in the next chapter, a flow of investment capital to the South. In terms of gross fixed capital formation, for the period 1995–2008 government investment was, on average, higher than that of the EU 15, and comparable to that of Ireland and Spain, while private investment was also higher than the EU 15 level, but below that of Spain (see Table 2.1).

Table 2.1   Gross fixed capital formation (% GDP)

	Greece	EU 15	Ireland	Spain
By type of goods				
Metal products and machinery	3.8	5.4	3.4	4.8
Transport equipment	3.1	1.9	2.7	2.3
Dwellings	9.6	5.7	9.2	9.5
Non-residential construction	4.4	5.6	6.5	8.3
By sector				
General government	3.3	2.4	3.5	3.5
Private sector	18.3	17.6	19.1	22.6

Sources: AMECO Database; authors' calculations.

Note: Numbers are 1995–2008 averages.

These were years, not only of high growth and investment, but high profits. As can be seen from Figure 2.5, profitability, as measured by the rate of return on capital, was on an upward trend throughout the period, even allowing for the fact that 1990 was a year of recession and for other cyclical variations. Given all the above, it seems that the conspiracy of sectional interests, tied to an inefficient state, was not as successful in denting the spirit of entrepreneurship and the values of production as has been claimed.

Thus, it is difficult to make the case that Greece as a whole was consuming more than it was producing. The charge of 'too much spending' is one that was to be, after the crisis, levelled at many economies and not just Greece. As Skidelsky (2011) argues, with respect to the US, there is always some truth to the Hayekian argument that cheap credit can lead to too much, or misdirected, investment, which may in turn lead to unsustainable levels of consumption. But

this is not the same as saying that there was overinvestment in the strict sense that further investment would have yielded a zero rate

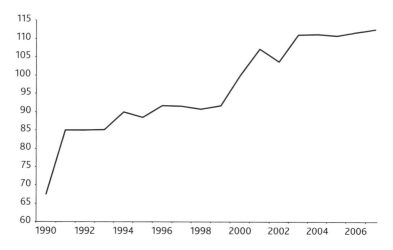

Figure 2.5   Net returns on net capital stock (2000 = 100)

Source: own calculations from AMECO database and National Statistical Service of Greece.

of return, or that there was too much consumption in general. It is absurd to believe that the demand for goods and services of those 46 million Americans living below the poverty line had reached the point of saturation. The houses and construction facilities built in the bubble economy are still there: they require an increase, not a reduction, in the incomes of the low-paid in order to become 'affordable'.

We shall return to the issue of poverty and inequality, which tends to be obscured by talk of too much spending. For the moment we need to concede that in this period savings rates did fall in Greece.[29] But care needs to be taken so that aggregate figures do not obscure important distributional issues. Financial deregulation in Greece increased the opportunities for borrowing (either for house purchases or general consumption), and bank credit to households exhibited rates in excess of 30 per cent per annum until the crisis. This led to a build-up of household debt, which reached just over 50 per cent of GDP by March 2010 (still below the euro area average). However, results of household surveys conducted by the Bank of Greece (in 2002, 2005 and 2007) suggest that only about 50 per cent of households in Greece have some kind of debt obligation (including loans from friends or other family members). Moreover, Simigiannis and Tzamourani (2007) show that the probability of having debt is strongly positively related to income. This suggests that, while financial liberalization in Greece helped to support the emergence of a new middle class, significant sections of society remained unaffected – they did not have access to loans. It was not possible, therefore, to satisfy their aspirations through the accumulation of debt as witnessed in the Anglo-Saxon economies.[30]

As in the US, a case can be made for misdirected investment. From Table 2.1 we can glean that for the period 1995–2008, and compared with the EU 15, investments were more concentrated in construction and transport (buses and trams) and much less in metals and machinery. Needless to say, the construction boom hardly consisted of social housing on the model of earlier social-democratic experiments in Northern Europe, while the Greek experience does not diverge significantly from that of the other PIGS (Portugal, Ireland and Spain). Here too, any discussion of the quality of investment can hardly avoid the issue of social inequality.

Another problematic feature was the reluctance of the private sector to invest in research and developement. Here the Greek experience diverges not just from European averages, but from other economies in the South.

There is a case to be made for short-termism in Greek capitalism in the years before the crisis. Left-wing economists, such as Yiannis

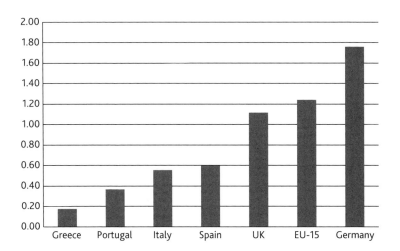

Figure 2.6   R&D expenditure in the business enterprise sector (% GDP)

Source: EUROSTAT, Statistics on Research and Development.

Note: Numbers are 2000–08 averages.

Dragasakis (2012), had been arguing from the time of Greece's accession to the Eurozone in 2001, that the nominal convergence achieved disguised a serious deficit with respect to real convergence. Greek business and financial elites were interested in short-term profits; and as we shall see in the next chapter, cheap money, European structural funds, as well as plentiful supplies of cheap immigrant labour, provided an excellent environment for this pursuit. In this context there was little interest in reinvesting these profits to create a common pool of infrastructural, skills-based and other common resources. Nor was modernizing the state a priority: for elites the confusion or inefficiency of the state was more likely to provide an opportunity than to be seen as an obstacle.

But dissenting voices were whistling in the wind while the going, and profits, were good. The charge of short-termism will in any case be familiar to readers in many countries, especially in the more liberal ones.[31] Since Ottoman times Greece has been a low-trust society. The arbitrariness of state power, the role of clientelistic politics and the importance of contacts that are 'here today and gone tomorrow' have not provided a suitable environment for long-term commitments. The relative weight in the overall economy of somewhat footloose shipping and finance partly reflects this state of affairs (Lyberaki and Tsakalotos, 2002). It was not a framework that was easily addressed given the neoliberal frame of mind of most modernizers. As elsewhere, the emphasis on individualism and entrepreneurship encouraged activities that were parasitic on, and destructive of, the common frameworks upon which all economies rely. Modernizers are not, on the whole, susceptible to Polanyian insights and sensitivities.[32]

The Polanyian theme of underinvestment in a common framework was a charge that could be heard throughout the neoliberal world in this period. The same could be said with respect to the presence of structural problems: angst about deindustrialization has been a permanent feature of the policy landscape; in the case of the UK since World War I, and of the US since World War II. Overall, then, it is difficult to make the case that the failings of the Greek economy were the result of an insufficient dose of the required neoliberal medicine. Indeed, the opposite assertion may be closer to home. To take just one example, the growth of finance did not lead to funds going to where they were most needed. They also funded a consumer boom, a bubble in the stock market that ended in tears in the early autumn of 1999, and a real estate bubble. None of these phenomena were as extreme as elsewhere, in Spain and Ireland for instance, but they have their place in the overall story. It is not one that is out-of-step with developments in the same period elsewhere.

It is not even clear what the relevant counterfactual is in many of the criticisms levelled at the Greek economy from a neoliberal or modernizing perspective. After all, within the EU, industrial policy, directed credit and many other aspects of Ha-Joon Chang's (2002) ladder had long been 'kicked away'. The belief that a smaller state, and a more neoliberal economy, could have resolved the tendency towards short-termism and the other structural problems of Greek economy, is not supported by the general experience of neoliberal economies elsewhere. The fact that the world economic crisis began in the more liberal economies is one more inconvenient fact for the dominant narrative.

SOCIAL STRUCTURE

It could be argued that so far we have been concentrating too much on the surface of things – that underneath the success story of growth and expansion there lay deep-rooted fault lines within the social structure that were bound to come to the surface sooner or later. Maybe this is the place to look for evidence for Greece's supposed underdevelopment. The size of the Greek state, the nature of the labour force and the persistence of small firms are three features of the Greek social formation that are usually referred to in this context.

The influential modernizing journalist, of the right-wing *Kathemerini*, Paschos Mandravelis was prone to portray the Greek crisis when it broke as one of the state, or even of socialism. There is no question that public sector employment has been a crucial element in clientelistic politics, with such employment constituting a central aspiration for many middle- and working-class families.[33] But the claims about the resulting size of the state have been much exaggerated, both before and after the crisis, both within and outside Greece. To be sure, state employment as a share of total employment is higher in Greece than in Germany, Spain or Italy, although much smaller than in Scandinavian countries (see Figure 2.7).

In a context of an underdeveloped welfare state, and a financial system that was not, as we have seen, yet in a position to lend to the bottom half of the income distribution, this is perhaps unsurprising. All capitalist social formations need mechanisms to spread the gains of the market to some less privileged social groups, and the clientelistic state was the preferred option of elites in Greece. But

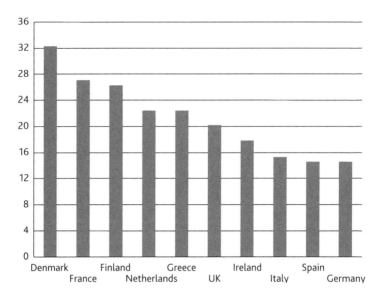

Figure 2.7   Public sector employment in selected EU countries, as a share of total employment (2008)

Source: ILO, Laborsta Database, http://laborsta.ilo.org/ (accessed May 2013).

Notes: Data are for 2006 for France, 2005 for the Netherlands and 2004 for the UK. Public sector employment covers employment in general government and public corporations.

again, one should not exaggerate. In terms of primary government expenditure Greece is below not only the Scandinavian economies, but those of Southern Europe as well (see Figure 2.8).

There are issues to be discussed: regarding the quality of state services, to which we shall return shortly; and the composition of state expenditure, which we shall take up in Chapter 4. But the size of the state in Greece does not seem to be such that it can carry much explanatory weight in any narrative concerning the crisis. For, as we argued in Chapter 1, neoliberals do not oppose the state in general, but a particular form of the state. This does not preclude some commitment with respect to size. However, in most neoliberal experiments this commitment has not always been easily adhered to: both for objective reasons that have to do with the contradictions of a market economy, but also because the size of the state has often become the locus of all those rearguard actions within both the parties of the centre-right and the centre-left (and of course from outside the consensus as well) that have sought to provide some resistance to the overall direction of policy.

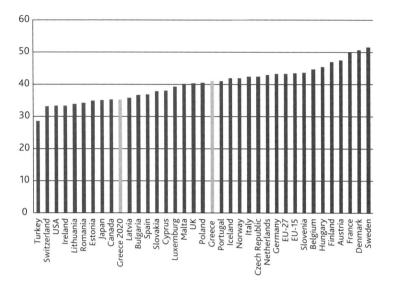

Figure 2.8 Total primary general government expenditure (% GDP)

Sources: AMECO Database and IMF.

Notes: For all countries, bars show the average primary expenditure as % of GDP for the years 2000–08 (2006–08 for Turkey). The value for Greece in 2020 is taken from IMF (15 February 2012) 'Greece: Preliminary Debt Sustainability Analysis', Table 1.

Moving on to the private sector, employment in the primary and secondary sectors amounts to 33.2 per cent of total employment, as compared to 28.7 per cent in the EU 15 (see Table 2.2). So the idea that Greece is skewed towards services is also not borne out by the facts.

Nor does the myth of work-shy Greek workers have any supporting empirical backing (see Figure 2.9).

What does seem exceptional is the extent of self-employment (Figure 2.10). Excluding Italy, the EU is characterized by the predominance of wage labour, with Germany leading the way with nine out of ten workers employed as wage earners. Greece's high level of self-employment is, however, slightly distorted by the extent of self-employment in the agricultural sector (compare columns 1 and 4, in Table 2.3). Moreover, Greece's exceptionalism has been on the decrease. The gap between Greek and EU 15 levels has fallen from about 30 percentage points (48.5 per cent and 18 per cent, respectively) in 1974 to about half that number by 2008 (35 per cent and 14 per cent). Interestingly, as the Italian level has changed

Table 2.2 Employment by sector (% total employment)

	Greece	EU 15
Primary sector	11.1	3.1
Manufacturing and construction	22.1	25.6
Services	66.7	71.3

Sources: EUROSTAT; authors' calculations.

Notes: Data refer to 2008. Percentages do not add up to 100 per cent due to rounding. Grouping of sectors based on NACE Rev.2: (1) Primary sector: agriculture, forestry and fishing; mining and quarrying. (2) Manufacturing and construction: manufacturing; electricity, gas, steam and air conditioning supply; water supply; sewerage, waste management and remediation activities; construction. (3) Services: wholesale and retail trade; repair of motor vehicles and motorcycles; transportation and storage; accommodation and food service activities; information and communication; financial and insurance activities; real estate activities; professional, scientific and technical activities; administrative and support service activities; public administration and defence; compulsory social security; education; human health and social work activities; arts, entertainment and recreation; other service activities; activities of households as employers; undifferentiated goods and services producing activities of households for own use; activities of extraterritorial organizations and bodies.

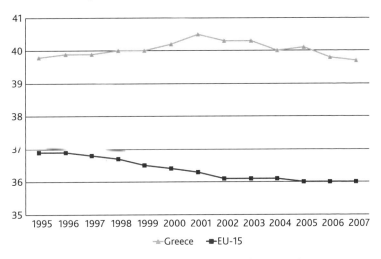

Figure 2.9 Average number of usual weekly hours of work in main job

Sources: EUROSTAT, European Labour Force Surveys.
Notes: Data refer to employees only, and include paid and unpaid overtime.

very little, Greece's divergence from Italy has fallen from 20 to 10 percentage points during the same period.

But we can go further, for some of those characterized as self-employed are in reality disguised wage-labourers doing a modern version of piece-work (Kouzis, 2007). Increased levels of

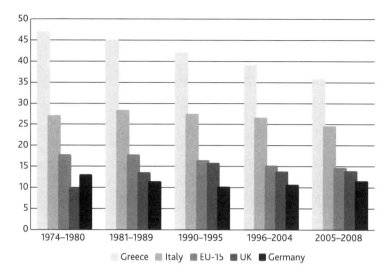

Figure 2.10   Self-employment in Greece and selected EU Countries
(% total employment)

Source: AMECO Database.

Table 2.3   Self-employment in the agricultural and non-agricultural sectors (2008)

	(1) Self-employment	(2) Employment in the agricultural sector	(3) Self-employment in the agricultural sector	(4) Self-employment in the non-agricultural sector
Greece	34.9	11.3	84.6	28.6
Germany	11	2.1	47.6	10.2
Italy	23.6	3.9	46.2	22.7
UK	13.3	1.5	45.9	12.8

Sources: OECD Structural Analysis (STAN) Databases, http://stats.oecd.org/Index.aspx (accessed May 2013); authors' calculations.

Notes: (1) Self-employed as % of total employment. (2) Employed in the agricultural sector as % of total employment. (3) Self-employed in the agricultural sector as % of total employment in the agricultural sector. (4) Self-employed in the non-agricultural sector as % of total employment in the non-agricultural sector.

labour market flexibility, promoted by all modernizing administrations (see Chapter 1), have led to a situation in which large numbers of technicians, engineers, plumbers, accountants and others work for a specific employer, or group of employers, but are paid by the specific service offered. If to this group we add those doctors, engineers and lawyers that work for large concerns (hospitals, law offices, etc.), then the share of the genuinely self-employed could fall by a further 5 percentage points. And, of course, employers, in both the private and public sector, gain by not having to pay for social security contributions, holidays and so on. Thus many of the 'self-employed' are, if anything, even more exploited than many workers in the private sector; part of a long-standing neoliberal trend in which transfers of risk to those least able to bear it are disguised as productivity gains. What needs to be underlined is that such trends can hardly be used as evidence for the underdevelopment, and insufficiently capitalist nature, of the Greek economy.

Table 2.4   Employment by establishment size (% of total employment)

	2005		2010	
	Greece	EU 15	Greece	EU 15
1 employee	14.8	10.2	20.1	11
2–9 employees	42.1	26.2	38.6	30.1
10–49 employees	25.7	28.3	25.5	27.6
50–249 employees	10.2	19.4	10.8	18.8
250+ employees	7.3	15.8	5.1	12.5

Source: European Working Conditions Survey 2005 and 2010; authors' calculations.

Notes: (1) Sample sizes for 2005: 985 for Greece, 14,357 for EU 15; for 2010: 1,027 for Greece, 21,731 for EU 15. (2) The corresponding questions in the two survey years are: 'Q6. How many people in total work in the local unit of the establishment where you work?' in 2005 and 'Q11. How many people in total work at your workplace (at the local site)?' in 2010. (3) Survey weights are used. (4) Percentages do not add up to 100 per cent due to rounding.

What about the prevalence of small firms? It is certainly the case that Greek workers work, on the whole, for small enterprises (see Table 2.4). In 2002, of 879,318 firms in all forms of economic activity, 844,917, or 96.1 per cent of the total, employed between one and four employees (Laskos and Tsakalotos, 2012: 62). Only 16–17 per cent of the labour force is employed in establishments with over 50 employees, compared to an EU average of between 30 per cent and 35 per cent (Table 2.4). The persistence of small enterprises is not only to be explained in terms of Greece's economic historical development, let alone its culture.[34] For the political scientist Gerasimos Moschonas, the incentive structures of the Greek state, even in the period of modernization, systematically worked against wage employment in the private sector and in favour of employment in the public sector and setting up a small business.[35] With respect to the latter, a large part of the story has to do with the ability of small firms to avoid paying taxes and social security contributions, an issue to which we will return when discussing the link between tax evasion and the fiscal crisis of the state.

For the moment we need to stress that while there is an argument to be had concerning the advantages and disadvantages of such a divergence from European norms, it is not clear that the dominance of the small firm makes the Greek economy any less capitalist, or less neoliberal.[36]

THE SOCIAL DEFICIT

Given that the modernizing drive from the mid-1990s onwards was mostly under the auspices of the centre-left party, PASOK, what is surprising is that so little was done to address the legacy of Greece's authoritarian past on social injustices of all types. If there was a major failure during the good times, it was surely this.

Inequality remained high in the whole period. By 2008, as measured by the Gini coefficient, Greece had the most unequal income distribution amongst the EU 15, bar Portugal and the UK. Things get worse with respect to poverty, where Greece stands in pole position (see Figures 2.11 and 2.12). It is true to say that in

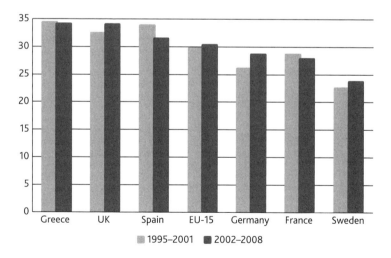

Figure 2.11   Income inequality – Gini coefficient

Sources: EUROSTAT; EU-SILC.

Notes: A higher value of the coefficient represents a more unequal distribution of income. Data expressed as period averages.

this period there was no sharp deterioration in social injustice, compared to trends in the more liberal economies for instance, but given the highly unacceptable starting position this hardly amounts to a major achievement.

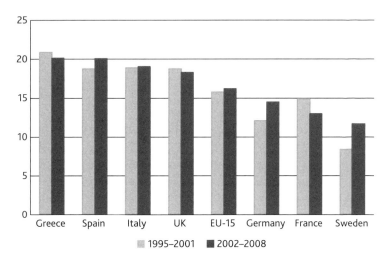

Figure 2.12 At-risk-of-poverty rate (%)

Sources: EUROSTAT; EU-SILC.

Notes: Percentage of people with less than 60 per cent of median equivalized income after social transfers. Data expressed as period averages.

If this period is really to be characterized as one in which pie redistribution always trumped pie growth, then there is precious little to show for all the effort involved. True, expenditure on pensions did converge on European levels, and this did help reduce the risk of entering into poverty. But other social expenditure did not (see Figures 2.13 and 2.14). In general, Greece is more generous than the EU average with respect to social expenditure that excludes social transfers in kind. But if we take both types, Greece spends below EU averages.[37] Moreover, apart from pensions, social expenditure was much less effective than elsewhere in Europe in reducing the risk of poverty for many sections of society (Matsaganis, 2011).

At the same time, the sense of social injustice was reinforced by the developments in the labour market already discussed. Greek workers were not well protected and unemployment benefit was meager and difficult to acquire (see Tables 2.5 and 2.6).

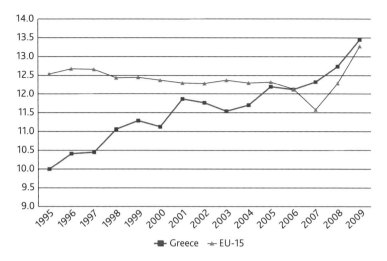

Figure 2.13   Pensions expenditure (% GDP)

Source: EUROSTAT.

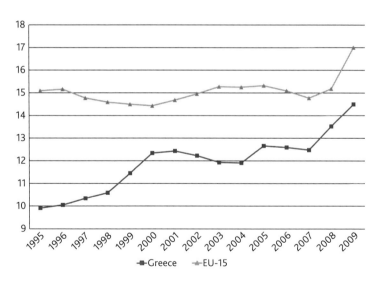

Figure 2.14   Social expenditure excluding pensions (% GDP)

Sources: EUROSTAT; authors' calculations.

Note: Data calculated by subtracting pensions expenditure (% of GDP) from total social expenditure (% of GDP).

Table 2.5   Strictness of employment protection legislation – regular employment (2000–2008)

Portugal	4.24
Germany	2.86
Spain	2.51
France	2.46
EU 15	**2.37**
Greece	**2.3**
Italy	1.77
Denmark	1.63
Ireland	1.6
UK	1.12

Source: OECD Indicators of Employment Protection (http://www.oecd.org/employment/ protection – accessed May 2013).

Notes: Data are for version 1 of the OECD index for the strictness of EPL regarding regular employment, and is the average for the years 2000–2008. The EU 15 value is the average of the values for the EU 15 countries.

Table 2.6   Gross unemployment benefit replacement rate (1999–2007)

Denmark	52
Portugal	42
France	40
Spain	36
EU 15	**34**
Italy	33
Ireland	32
Germany	27
Greece	**14**

Source: Benefits and Wages: OECD Indicators (http://www.oecd.org/els/social/workincentives – accessed May 2013).

Notes: The table presents the OECD summary measure of benefit entitlements, defined as the average of the gross unemployment benefit replacement rates for two earnings levels, three family situations and three durations of unemployment for each country. Data are the averages for the 1999–2007 values for each country. The EU 15 value is the average of the values for the EU 15 countries.

In other words, the modernizing drive of Kostas Simitis, and his two PASOK administrations, did not entail anything like a new social contract. Social democrats in the corporatist era had recognized the existence of the 'interpretations gap':[38] workers were often called upon to make sacrifices now, in exchange for gains at some later date. But in a market economy, what is the guarantee that such gains will be distributed when the time comes? Corporatism, and enhancing the institutional power of workers in general, was seen as a response to this problem. But for the modernizers of Simitis, such power could only reinforce the forces of sectionalism that were the main enemies of reform.

The failure to do more to reform pensions must be seen in this light. The Left, and PASOK-dominated unions, were able to block the Giannitsis reform in the early 2000s, and water down most (but by no means all) other initiatives on this front. For modernizers of all persuasions, and not just those associated with PASOK, this constituted a key turning point in the modernizing project as a whole – in the years after the crisis, leftist opposition to austerity would be condemned for its sterile negativity, and be met with the charge that if pension reform had been addressed more successfully earlier, there would not have been the need for such tough austerity measures.

But it was not as if modernizers could promise that movement on this front could be chalked off with progressive social initiatives elsewhere. For all sides were agreed that the Greek pension system was complex and that the winners of the system were not always those with the most need; although, as we have seen, and in con-tradistinction to other social spending, it did reduce the risk of poverty. However, after the mid-1990s the only promise on offer was that a more stable fiscal regime, in part through cutting pension costs, and a more flexible market economy would eventually raise the prospects for all and not just the immediate winners. But it cannot be said that 'trickle down' economics have fared very well in the neoliberal period (Quiggin, 2010: chapter 4). Workers and pensioners were rightly suspicious, and their actions seem all too rational, and not out of step with rearguard actions in other countries during the same period.

There is a bottom line here: Greece, at the beginning of the period of the metapolitefsi in 1974, started off with one of the most unequal income distributions and with the highest levels of poverty in the EU. By 2009 this was still the case. In short, Greek elites had more than held their own. The social issue was to become explosive material once the crisis developed and the policies of austerity began to be implemented. The parties of the centre-left and centre-right were seen to be abandoning their social base. But it was a process that had begun well before 2008.

CORRUPTION AND THE DEMOCRATIC DEFICIT

If the years of growth were not used to address either some of Greece's structural economic problems or the social deficit, then the same could be said for the democratic deficit. If anything the failure here was even more evident, and for modernizers more glaring, given that the overhaul of the political system was presented as an outright priority and a prerequisite for nearly all other reforms. Yet the last two pre-crisis administrations ended, under PASOK in 2004 and New Democracy in 2009, with a series of allegations of political scandals (see Appendix). For modernizers, whose proclivity for self-criticism can hardly count as one of their stronger points, the failure to rid political life of corrupt practices and imbue the political system with a greater dose of transparency can be laid at the door of the usual suspects who had run Greece's political system, at least since the metapolitefsi. There is little awareness of the fact that corruption has been a permanent feature of the neoliberal era worldwide.

Part of the problem was the fact that the dominant narrative does not conceive the problem as being one of insufficient democracy. Its analysis of Greece's woes has strong links to the public choice critique of the social-democratic consensus that started growing in the advanced capitalist economies in the 1960s. Mancur Olson (1965) and James Buchanan and Gordon Tullock (1962), employing the individualistic theoretical toolbox of neoclassical economics, addressed the issue of how politics could distort the preferences of individuals and lead to a multitude of inefficiencies. Thus distribution coalitions, with an interest in increasing their share of the pie, could gang up on those productive coalitions that society needs in order to increase the pie. At the same time politicians and bureaucrats, who like all other agents in the economy act out of pure self-interest, have every reason to come to terms with sectionalist interests. The resulting 'democratic overload' can only store up problems for the future, usually materializing as a fiscal crisis of the state.

Such an approach found strong echoes in explanations of the Greek clientelistic state: the exchange of favours known as rousfeti, the use of public sector employment to build up political coalitions, and the lack of transparency in public procurements and the choice of public investment projects which were at the heart of the spectacular political scandals that broke out in the pre-crisis period. But there is a danger in employing academic, and overtly political, literature out of context.[39] For public choice theorists were responding to the rise of the social-democratic state, the strength of unions, and the existence of various forms of industrial democracy that were developed post-World War II in the economies of advanced capitalism. Moreover, these institutions had been associated with a much more equal income distribution until the late 1960s; what Paul Krugman has called the era of the Great Compression.

But, as we have seen, in post-1974 Greece experiments in social levelling and democratic deepening were half-hearted in conceptualization and limited in outcome. The clientelistic phenomenon was, in other words, far from being a problem of democratic overload.[40] On the contrary, by building strong vertical links between political parties or individual politicians on the one hand, and individual voters or special interests on the other, there was an undercutting of horizontal organizations that form the backbone of democracy and can, at their best, mitigate elite power. As David Putnam (1993) has argued, in the case of Italy, the hierarchical relations of clientelism rely on and reinforce the values of self-interest and opportunism. It is not clear in this context, then, to what extent the neoliberal strategy of expanding the market domain, and thus also that of self-interest, can provide a coherent response.

And indeed no coherent response was in evidence in the years after 1996. The modernizers of PASOK attempted to implement some measures to increase transparency. Thus Anastasios Peponis, a prominent PASOK politician of the old guard, passed a law in 1994 (subsequently known as the Peponis Law) that attempted to organize public sector appointments through some kind of objective criteria. This met with partial success, although in a low-trust society, or where the spirit of public service rarely manages to trump self-interest, such interventions can always be bypassed. All too often they handicap the honest through increased red tape, without unduly troubling the dishonest who have, in any case, built up considerable expertise in bypassing rules and regulations.

Greece has been overburdened by laws since the nineteenth century, which simply add to existing legislation without any attempt to simplify the legal minefield thus created. In this light most modernizing administrations tried to bypass the public administration altogether, creating a parallel system of political advisors, policy experts and consultants. But instead of providing a breeding ground for new values and more transparent bureaucratic practices, the parallel system was all too easily incorporated into the standard practices of clientelistic politics.

The dominant narrative was well aware of these failures to challenge clientelistic and corrupt practices. International reports and rankings were duly disseminated to show how poorly Greece faired in these areas, and how this affected Greece's competitiveness and its attractiveness as a location for foreign direct investment (FDI). However, there was little awareness of the limitations of these rankings; for instance, their reliance on business perceptions of corruption, and the neglect of corruption in the private sector (Hodgson and Jiang, 2007). In any case, these reports and rankings were more useful in the ideological struggle to promote modernizing ideas than in providing any clear policy advice, other than persevering with the usual canopy of neoliberal reforms. As with the hope invested in trickle-down economics to sort out the social question, here there was a similarly sanguine expectation that more markets, liberalization and deregulation would gradually remove the grazing ground of corrupt practices.[41]

But as we now know, corruption seems to be eminently compatible with neoliberal politics: from phone hacking to politicians fiddling their expenses, from manilla envelopes for public procurements to accountants offering a light-touch audit in order not to lose other profitable business from the audited firm, from speculative financial activity to banks rigging interest rates, the list seems endless. As Quiggin (2000) argues, it is a paradox of our times that rent-seeking behaviour seems more prominent in the post-liberalization era.[42] What was never envisaged was that the answer could rest in increasing democracy and the level of democratic accountability. And yet in the period after World War II both corruption (Chibber, 2005) and social inequalities (Krugman, 2002) were mitigated through the rise of collective democratic institutions that limited the power of elites. However, as we have seen collective solutions are antithetical to the whole neoliberal way of thinking.

In this context, the fact that scandals dominated much of the political agenda in Greece in this period can hardly contribute to the case for Greek exceptionalism. In the Appendix we give a more detailed account of two characteristic scandals of the period. Both were to poison the atmosphere and bring politics in to disrepute. After 2010 they contributed to the political crisis that was inexorably linked to that of the economy.

CONCLUSION

On the eve of the crisis, the Greek economy had experienced a period of exceptionally good growth, and seen GDP per capita converge significantly on the EU average. Few in 2004 – the *annus mirabilis* of post-war Greece, when winning the European Cup and the Eurovision song contest ushered in the summer's Olympic Games – could have predicted the unfolding of subsequent events.

For the modernizing narrative the writing was already on the wall. The alarm bells should have been set off as a result of the persistent failure to come to grips with state finances, an issue we have left unexplored here as it forms a critical element of the crisis to be discussed in Chapter 4. But the narrative, we have seen, is defective in both the generalities and the particulars of economic and social developments since the mid-1990s. It is true to say that the 'good years' were not used in a way that dealt with the social and democratic deficit bequeathed by the early metapolitefsi period. It is also true that some, but only some, structural problems of the Greek economy proved remarkably persistent. But as we shall see in the following chapter, it is difficult to come to grips with the world and Eurozone crisis without incorporating into the story such social and democratic deficits, as well as significant structural economic problems.

In short, the case for Greek exceptionalism is unconvincing. Greek policy was impeccably neoliberal in intent, and the problems of society and the economy are best seen in terms of the contradictions of a particular example of neoliberalism. The problems lie with the nature of neoliberalism and capitalism, not underdevelopment and resistance to modernizing reforms, and it is to these problems that we now turn.

3
The Eurozone Crisis in Context

Greece's GDP amounts to about 2 per cent of the EU total; somewhere between Maryland and Indiana in US terms. And yet, from early 2010, Greece was rarely out of the international limelight, with countless European Councils and Eurogroup (finance ministers of the Eurozone) meetings focusing on its plight, but also on other countries that were to join, one after another, the downward spiral of debt and austerity. By 2011 and 2012, the issue had become the fate of the euro itself. It is difficult to believe that similar problems in either Maryland or Indiana could have sparked off such a crisis within the US. But to paraphrase E.H. Carr's (1961) impatience with accounts that elevate the role of accident in historical explanations, if the Greek crisis was so critical, there must be some underlying reasons for the susceptibility of the Eurozone economy to developments in Greece.

This chapter deals with this susceptibility and the wider canvas of the world economic crisis that began in 2008 with the financial crash. As hopes waned that the crisis would be overcome fairly swiftly, with what was then known as a V-shaped recovery[43] (in other words a sharp recovery following on from the steep fall in economic activity), it became obvious that the levels of world debt acquired during the preceding two decades were well beyond what could be justified by the growth performance. Consequently, people began to look more closely at indebted economies, and financial institutions, that were particularly at risk. They also began to question who would bear the main burden of readjustment.

It is in this context that long-standing worries about the economic and financial architecture of the Eurozone began to resurface. From before the creation of European monetary union there had been voices expressing considerable scepticism about whether the economies involved constituted an optimal currency area; that is, whether the cost of giving up the policy instrument of the exchange rate was really less than the benefits of adopting a single currency. The concern was accentuated by the fact that the architects had made no provision for a large federal budget, or other institutions for that matter, which could act as a stabilizer for regions doing less well than others, thereby injecting an element of solidarity in to the whole framework. The Greek crisis set such concerns in the sharpest possible focus: did the Eurozone have the commitment and the ability to act speedily to provide a collective solution to the emerging crisis of its periphery?

But the crisis, and the re-evaluation of economic performance that preceded it, also brought to the fore the future viability, not to mention desirability, of the neoliberal economic and social order as a whole. Towards the end of 2011, the *Financial Times* was running a series of articles on 'Capitalism in crisis', which it intended as 'An investigation into the future of capitalism scrutinising its legitimacy, its weaknesses and suggesting ways in which it could be reformed'. Such a venture would have been unthinkable five years earlier. Clearly something more serious was afoot than financial irresponsibility and the need for financial regulation. Part of our task here is to investigate the nature of this world crisis, as a prelude to examining the cases of the Eurozone and Greece.

A WORLD CRISIS OF MANY MOMENTS

In earlier work, we argued that neoliberalism is best seen as a response to the first major capitalist crisis of the post-World War II era, which was in evidence by the late 1960s as profit shares and rates began to decline, but which only fully materialized in the 1970s (Laskos and Tsakalotos, 2011). Capital and ruling elites were not just concerned with falling profits. The end of the 'Golden Age' of capitalism had seen various political tribulations that had brought to the fore challenges to the post-war consensus from a more radical direction, including factory occupations and experiments in self-management in France and Italy, and a shift to the Left in a number of social-democratic parties. The increasing turn to incomes policies to deal with the phenomenon of stagflation was also ambiguous from the perspective of capital: such policies had a tendency to open up the agenda of debate in the process of 'political exchange', and their effectiveness relied on bringing conflict into the open and making clear that the crisis would be solved not through a technocratic fix but through a social-political one with clear winners and losers (Goldthorpe, 1987). For political scientists, such as Maier and Lindberg (1985), one exit from the 1970s crisis entailed a deepening of the social-democratic consensus. It was not an exit that capital could look on with equanimity.

The other exit was the dismantling of that consensus in order to restore the class power of capital and place the economy onto a renewed path of dynamic capital accumulation. For David Harvey (2007), these were the two main objectives of the neoliberal project. The official rhetoric may have put the emphasis on free markets, but the reality is better understood by the four features introduced in Chapter 1: capital as the universal class, the regulating role of finance, opposition to a particular (Keynesian-social-democratic) state rather than the state in general, and hostility to all forms of collective action which attempt to redistribute resources to the losers of competition. Neoliberalism, too, entailed a social-political fix, with clear winners and losers.

Marx and Gramsci had both been aware that laissez-faire was far from being a natural state of affairs, or the default mode as we would now say, in the absence of political tinkering and the interventions of sectionalist interests. Instead, it is a programme that needs planning and organization, political initiatives and social mobilization. Neoliberal think-tanks, international conferences and political activity within centre-right parties, all lucratively funded by various private sector interests, were a feature even before the 1970s crisis, but they became even more influential from that point on. From the 1980s onwards neoliberals were in positions of power so as to promote their ideas. There followed a series of institutional interventions which all bolstered neoliberalism on a global level: liberalization of capital controls, liberalization of trade and services, and, of course, within Europe the process of integration through the single market programme and monetary union.

However, such interventions 'from above' were preceded or complimented by similar moves from below. Streeck (2011b) argues, in an exceptionally astute analysis of capitalist institutions that fuses Marxian and Polanyian elements, that it is in the nature of capitalism, through legitimizing self-interest and the profit motive, to see its existing institutions and social contracts being eroded by the actions of individuals and firms. Thus, well before the era of liberalized finance, American and other banks had managed to get around capital controls, as well as various interest rate and deposit regulations, through the Eurocurrency markets that blossomed from the late 1960s onwards (Gibson, 1989). At the same time, multinational companies (MNCs) were also eroding essential features of the post-war settlement through the practice of transfer pricing and their ability to shift vast resources across borders. So the era of globalization was ushered in by the dynamism of capital

– its tendency to stretch (if not bypass altogether) laws, social contracts, and existing traditions and practices, whether explicit or implicit. It is not a phenomenon that would surprise anyone with even a cursory acquaintance of Marx and Engel's portrayal of the dynamism of capital in the *Communist Manifesto*.

There can be no doubt that the neoliberal project was remarkably successful in its first goal of restoring the power of capital. The demise of union densities and the imposition of anti-union laws, the adoption of inflation as the number-one goal of macroeconomic policy and the explicit denial of government responsibility for full employment, the commodification of social goods and the attempts to rein in the welfare state, are only some of the symptoms of that shifting locus of power. Others will be discussed later. Capitalist class power had, by the 2000s, encompassed all three dimensions of Steven Lukes' (1975) definition: direct imposition, determination of the agenda and ideological hegemony.

What is perhaps more surprising is that success in the first goal did not lead to similar achievements with respect to the second. In terms of growth and productivity the results of the neoliberal era are, at best, mixed (see Table 3.1).

There is no question that the growth performance of the majority of advanced capitalist economies never replicated that of the Golden Age. For Western Europe, excluding the UK, growth is somewhere between what was achieved in the period before World War I and the interwar period. The UK and the US have been more consistent throughout the three periods, while there were pockets of growth in emerging economies – although more a clustering around different performance levels than a general catch-up as predicted by neoclassical trade theory (Quah, 1993). The picture for productivity growth in advanced capitalist economies is, if anything, more disappointing (see Figure 3.1).

For more neoclassical-orientated economists, the special features of the first post-World War II period could not be reproduced *ad infinitum*: the boost given by the post-war reconstruction effort, the successful catch-up of Western Europe to the US and the availability of plentiful supplies of labour (first from agriculture and then from immigration). This sounds like special pleading, and is in any case out-of-step with the predictions made by mainstream economists regarding the benefits that would follow from the implementation of the neoliberal programme. Many of those who subsequently accumulated debt must have, in part, believed these predictions.

Table 3.1 Longer-run GDP trends in Europe

	1870–1913 (a)	1922–37 (a)	1953–73 (a)	1973–79 (a)	1975–82 (a)	1983–92 (b)	1993–2008 (b)	1973–2008 (b)
UK	1.9	2.4	3	1.3	1.1	2.5	2.8	2.4
France	1.6	1.8	5.3	3.1	2.6	2.4	1.9	2.3
Germany	2.8	3.2	5.5	2.4	2.4	3.9	1.6	2.7
Italy	1.5	2.3	5.3	2.6	2.7	2.6	1.3	2.2
Spain	0.8	1.7	6.1	2.7	1.6	3.2	3.2	3
Austria	2.4	0.8	5.7	3	2.7	2.7	2.2	2.5
Belgium	2	1.4	4.3	2.4	1.8	2.3	2.2	2.3
Netherlands	1.9	1.9	4.9	2.4	1.5	2.8	2.7	2.5
Sweden	2.8	3.5	3.9	1.8	0.9	1.9	2.8	2.3
Western Europe excl. UK	2	2.5	5.1	2.6	2.3	2.8	2.1	2.4
US			3.3	3.4	2.4	3.5	3.9	3.4
Canada			5	4.1	2.6	2.7	3.5	3.2
Japan			8.6	4.2	4	3.8	0.9	2.5

Sources: (a) from Boltho, A. (1982) 'The European Economy', in D. Morris (ed.) *The Economic System in the UK*, 3rd edition, Oxford University Press; (b) own calculations from IMF International Financial Statistics data.

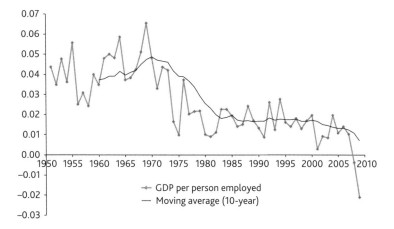

Figure 3.1   Labour productivity growth in advanced countries (GDP per person)

Source: Gronigen Total Economy Data Base (http://www.rug.nl/research/ggdc/ – accessed May 2013).

Heterodox and leftist economists are more divided on the issue. Some see a distinct failure in the whole exercise. Others have a more positive assessment, not only based on a different reading of the figures, but also because they see the spreading of a new economic capitalist regime throughout the world as a major achievement of capital in this period – one entitling us to speak in terms of a distinct autonomous regime of capitalist accumulation worldwide, and not just a failed episode in the attempt to overcome the crisis of the 1970s. A third group has a more nuanced approach, characterizing the neoliberal era as one of relative stagnation. Some of the difference depends on how one apportions the period of the 1970s, and that of the first recession that followed the monetarist experiments in the US and the UK in the early 1980s. Obviously, the neoliberal era looks rather better if these are excluded from its sphere of responsibility.

However, the 'relative stagnation' hypothesis is also supported by two other considerations. First, figures for profits do not support the idea of a new era of expanded reproduction. While profit shares recovered, as the attack on labour was successful, there was only a partial recovery in profit rates (Brenner, 2006; Duménil, G. and Lévy, 2010). Second, the existence of a savings glut contributed to the search for ever more exotic financial titles in which to invest. The line of causation here goes from poor profit rates (in part from the pressures of international competition) to the financialization process described below.

Whatever the overall assessment, and many of the issues remain unresolved, the neoliberal era ended in the crisis of 2008. Below we trace five interdependent processes that shed light on this second crisis of post-war capitalism.

Financial Liberalization

There have been periods of impressive globalization before in the history of capitalism (Hirst and Thompson, 1996). But what distinguished the latest episode was the explosion of short-term financial flows and the growth of manufacturing industries in less developed countries (Pollin, 2000). We begin with the first. The growth of international banking, the rise of international bond and security issues, and the explosion – there is no other word – in the turnover of foreign currency transactions is a process so well documented that we hardly need to reproduce the evidence here.

The first promise of financial liberalization was that efficiency would be promoted as financial resources were free to go to where they would be more useful – where the returns were highest. But the evidence is pretty clear on this matter: financial flows were largely determined by short-term speculative motives; that is to say, making a quick capital gain and moving on to the next profitable opening rather than a long-term commitment to a particular investment project.

Many economies faced large inflows of capital, and more dramatic outflows in some subsequent period, with the result that after liberalization exchange rate markets began more and more to resemble Keynes's beauty contest. This was most evident in the Southeast Asian financial crises during the second half of the 1990s, but the experience was common to Latin America, Russia and even within Europe in the early 1990s. Thus, the second promise of liberalization – financial stability – was fulfilled even less than the first. Indeed, a characteristic of the neoliberal era was not only the return of currency crises, after the relative lull of the Golden Age, but the ever-growing intensity of the phenomenon (Glyn, 2006; Krugman and Wells, 2011). But neither experience, nor common sense for that matter, can dent the enthusiasm of mainstream economists. Thus, only a few years before financial speculation wrecked the exchange rate mechanism (ERM) in Europe, Giavazzi and Pagano (1988) were explaining how the removal of capital controls actually increases the credibility of governments, and their commitment to a fixed exchange rate regime, thereby reducing the probability of a speculative attack.

Part of the problem is, no doubt, that the term 'financial liberalization' was stretched by neoliberal advocates to encompass a number of distinct issues. Gibson and Tsakalotos (1994), in their review of the financial liberalization literature, argue that financial repression (the problem that liberalization was purportedly seeking to address) tended to be a catch-all category that conflated different mechanisms and institutions. Thus, getting rid of fixed interest rates, which may have a negative effect on savings and growth, is a very different matter from prohibiting allocated credit for particular industries or winding down state development banks. Indeed, the latter have proved of considerable help to many emerging economies in their drive to industrialize (Chang, 2002). The result was that financial liberalization often set the development process back in many less developed countries (LDCs), and many economies (not just in the developing world) became increasingly vulnerable to financial instability (Glyn, 2006).

The age of the 'Great Moderation', as pronounced by Ben Bernanke, in which Gordon Brown could claim 'boom and bust' were banished, did not extend to the financial system.

The Liberalization of Trade

Liberalization of trade was on the agenda well before the rise of the neoliberal era. Indeed, the whole process of successive GATT (General Agreement on Tariffs and Trade) rounds was what the Americans extracted in the negotiations at the Bretton Woods conference in 1944, as a quid pro quo for accepting what they saw as the more Keynesian elements of the International Monetary Find (IMF). This more liberal element was enhanced with the onset of the neoliberal era, with the Uruguay Round (1986–94) being undoubtedly the most ambitious exercise in trade liberalization, extending the principle to textiles, agriculture, services and intellectual property rights. The screw was tightened further in 1995 with the creation of the World Trade Organization (WTO): an independent institution, replacing the previous rule-based approach in which the rules had to be agreed to by all the participating parties. It is no accident that the alter-globalization movements started shortly after the setting up of the WTO and the financial crises in Southeast Asia. Globalization had started in industry, but the dynamism of capitalism could not possibly leave it at that.

Within Europe, the Single European Act was working in the same direction. The Cecchini report in 1988, which ushered in the whole process, promised not only one-off gains from the removal of tariff and non-tariff barriers, but dynamic effects, permanently placing European economies on a higher-growth path. As we shall see, these never materialized. But of equal importance was the sidelining of distributional issues. Orthodox trade economics in general, and the economics of customs unions in particular, are not on the whole good at getting at these issues: the idea seems to be that liberalized trade can maximize global output, and the issue of distribution is a secondary matter – one for politics to sort out at some later date. But these distributional issues were to prove integral to the crisis of the Eurozone.

In the developing world, the rise in manufacturing shares was a genuinely important new development. But this rise in industrial production did not translate into an equally impressive rise in industrial employment for three reasons (Pollin, 2000). Firstly, the emphasis on export production, a critical element of the Washington neoliberal consensus, had its limits, as there are clear fallacy-of-composition elements – not all economies can base themselves on exports at the expense of imports. Secondly, many economies that turned to a strategy of export-led growth merely employed workers previously working in the import-substitution sector. Thirdly, the increase in productivity also played a role. For Pollin then, all these factors represent the return of the 'Marx problem'; with unemployment, underemployment and the informal economy constituting a vast reserve army of labour on a global scale, putting downward pressure on real wages in both developing and developed economies, and resulting in declining labour shares (in national income) throughout the world. For the flipside of industrialization in the developing world was not only deindustrialization, but also the heightened credibility of relocation threats by business in the economies of advanced capitalism.

Globalization, through financial and trade liberalization, does not mean that the nation state becomes of secondary importance, its powers dwarfed by the power of MNCs and financial markets (Panitch and Gindin, 2012). Foreign capital invested in a particular national social formation tends to become integrated (to varying degrees but to some extent everywhere) within that social formation. Moreover, international capital markets do not just work in favour of international capital in general, but also to strengthen the hand of ruling elites within particular national social formations. They act, in other words, not so much to alter the distribution of power against states, but to influence the distribution within states. These observations put some meat on our previous proposition that it is a misconception to see neoliberalism as opposing the state as such. The nation state in the era of globalization continues to provide the social, political and economic prerequisites for capitalist reproduction. This aspect is important to keep in mind when we go on to discuss the rise of inequalities and the hollowing out of democracy below, the role of the IMF in Greece in Chapter 4, and Left alternative strategies in Chapter 6.

Financialization

The role of financialization in the neoliberal economy has also been well documented, but important differences remain with respect to its interpretation.[44] It is a complex and multidimensional phenomenon not confined to the economic sphere, as the growing relative weight of finance bears heavily on the lives of ordinary citizens.

The growth in the financial sector is perhaps the outstanding characteristic of the whole period. Thus, by 2007 US profits in the financial sector were around 40 per cent of total profits of the corporate sector – the equivalent figure in 1980 had been about 10 per cent (Quiggin, 2010: 46). Less liberal economies could not match such an expansion, but similar trends could be observed in most places. These trends were underpinned by important institutional developments. For instance, firms were increasingly reliant on borrowing from capital markets rather than from banks, with larger enterprises able to issue their own bonds in international capital markets.

This shift symbolized the emerging, if partial, victory of the Anglo-Saxon style of finance over the German–Japanese one.[45] Within Europe, for instance, this shift was explicitly promoted by the European Commission, as a central plank of its strategy of enforcing a common market for financial services (Gibson and Tsakalotos, 2003). The main difference between the two lies in the length and the quality of the relationship between firms and the financial sector.[46] The German–Japanese model allows for more long-term relationships of trust and cooperation, in which firms do not have to focus on short-term profits, and can rely on banks for financing and other forms of assistance even in bad times. In terms of Albert Hirschman's distinction, there is a greater reliance on voice rather than on exit.

In the Anglo-Saxon model, on the other hand, corporate control shifts from banks to impersonal capital markets, with exit correspondingly having a greater role: it is the fear that shareholders may respond to poor performance, by selling their shares and thereby increasing the probability of hostile takeover, which is supposed to keep managers on their toes. The maximization of shareholder value becomes the central concern for managers; to the detriment, critics would argue, of other 'stakeholders' in the business such as workers, suppliers, customers and the wider community in which the firms operate. Moreover, given the incentive structures faced by pension and investment fund managers, who operate in a competitive environment with multiple options in which to invest, there is pressure on managers of firms to show short-term profits even if this means sacrificing more long-term investments. The accusation of short-termism was a constant refrain of critics of more liberal capitalism in the years before the crisis (Hutton, 1996), but could be comfortably ignored as long as stock markets were rising and dividends were being distributed.

Whatever the merits of the short-termism argument, to which we shall return, the corporate control aspects of the Anglo-Saxon model suggest that it is an exaggeration to identify financialization with speculative activity (Milios and Sotiropoulos, 2009). For in this model the role of finance becomes one of regulation and supervision, not only of capitalist firms, but of whole economies. Those firms, or economies, seen as not implementing the appropriate measures to maximize shareholder value, or not pursuing institutional reform to maximize profits on a wider scale, would see their shares, or bonds, sold off, with the result that their prices would fall and the cost of borrowing would increase. Finance was thus far more integrated within the 'real economy' than many accounts allow for (Konings and Panitch, 2008).

That having been said, one should not bend the stick too far the other way. For if the role of finance is to supervise firms, the question arises of who shall supervise the supervisors. And it cannot be said that the neoliberal order ever gave any very convincing answer to this question. The failure, then, to regulate the financial system in the period before the crisis did lead to a great deal of speculative activity that had little to do with either supervision or the needs of the real economy. Thus we agree with Ben Fine's (2010: 1) argument that one aspect of financialization 'can be understood in classical Marxist terms as the increasing appropriation of economic and social activity by dysfunctional forms of finance in which the appropriation of surplus takes undue, even some sort of systemic, precedence over its creation'.

However, what this does not mean is that the interests of finance and industry can be prised apart, as part of an alternative economic strategy of the Left. For the growing interpenetration of finance and industry is a concrete reality, the extent of speculative activity notwithstanding.[47] This interpenetration was solidified by the growing tendency of non-financial firms (such as General Motors, ENRON or General Electric) to make a sizeable share of their profits from essentially financial-type activities. One needs only to think about the average advertisement for cars, in which only half the time is apportioned to selling the product or perhaps the appropriate lifestyle conducive to purchasing it, while the other half is on the enticing credit conditions accompanying the purchase.

But financialization went beyond all this. It encompassed large sections of the population who had every reason to care about the outcome of the financial system, and stock markets, since their pensions, mortgages and personal loans were increasingly at stake. Getting one's finances in order was now a consideration for students with loans, young couples with mortgages, and even toddlers who had parents and other relatives participating in various financing schemes for their future. In this context financialization could not avoid having a cultural impact: the rise of a more dynamic and individualistic worldview – one in which the search for a quick gain was, with a slight exaggeration at this point, a pressing concern for all and sundry.

Before the crisis many leftist commentators were impressed by the raw power of this new zeitgeist. Perry Anderson (2002: 25), for instance, related US hegemony to the fact that it lacked the institutions of social embeddedness found in more institutional varieties of capitalism:

> unencumbered property rights, untrammelled litigation, the invention of the corporation. Here too, the result was the creation of what Polanyi most feared, a juridical system disembedding the market as far as possible from ties of custom, tradition or solidarity, whose very abstraction from them later proved – American firms like American films – exportable and reducible across the world, in a way that no other competitor could quite match.

For John Grahl (2001: 30) the battle between the more embedded bank-based systems and its more institutional rivals had been 'already lost and won'; for however efficient were the latter 'on a local basis ... [they] remain imprisoned in their specific social environments'. The more 'abstract' will tend to win over the more embedded, an evaluation that gained much support from the evidence of convergence between the various institutional forms of capitalism (Howell, 2003).[48]

However, what succeeds clearly depends on the environment in which it operates.[49] And the environment in this period was clearly skewed to the selection of more market-based solutions (Gowan, 1999). Even if they are not more efficient overall, more market-orientated practices (in the absence of remedial action) can drive out others. Thus Mayer (1994) argues that commitment lending is very vulnerable to competition from market-based sources of finance. If committed lenders are to see firms through both good and bad times, then they expect the lower returns received in bad times to be made up for by a better return in good times. However, in good times it is easier for firms to get finance from markets, and since this will be cheaper the incentive for firms to renege on the commitment relationship is great.

We have good grounds to question the superior economic efficiency of the more liberal economic model.[50] For instance, many takeovers were motivated by, and led to, the breaking of implicit contracts and cooperative agreements between managers and the existing stakeholders of the firm; implying not a gain in overall efficiency but a redistribution from workers to the new owners of the firm (Shleifer and Summers, 1988). Such practices were a constant feature of cinema's critique of the age of financialization, even in the most commercial of films. Thus, in *Pretty Woman* the corporate raider and asset stripper, Edward Lewis (Richard Gere), has to be 'reformed' (and not only in matters of business) by Vivian (Julia Roberts); while Gordon Gekko (Michael Douglas), in *Wall Street*, has come to represent pure greed, not only of many private equity firms but of the period as a whole.

In addition, it cannot be said that the Anglo-Saxon-style financial systems are known for their generosity in providing funds either for small- or medium-sized enterprises (because the institutional investors that dominate financial markets find larger companies easier to follow) or for manufacturing companies (because they tend to be capital intensive and do not necessarily generate a lot of cash). Thus the European Commission's support for the Anglo-Saxon way had implications for developments in the periphery of the Eurozone – one more rung of the ladder was being kicked away, with obvious implications for the potential for catch-up (Gibson and Tsakalotos, 2003).

One last observation with respect to the dynamism and efficiency of the market model is in order, because it bears on the issue of the choice of development model, and its financing, to which we return in our final chapter. As O'Neill (1998: 139–40) argues that 'the market as a mode of coordination appears to foster forms of abstract codifiable knowledge at the expense of knowledge that is local and practical'. But this abstractness cannot be equated to superior efficiency – the epistemic value of knowledge is in no direct relation to its market value. For O'Neil, both the market and centralized planning ignore important information that come from intermediate institutions and associations, and this can be an important source of economic success for any economic alternative to capitalism.[51]

In light of all the above, financialization may be partly responsible for the disappointing economic performance of the neoliberal era. It is definitely true to say that capitalism does not necessarily have to rely on the 'cosy' cooperative and embedded variety for making profits – in more Marxist language, it can rely as much on the extraction of absolute as opposed to relative surplus value. But overall economic performance may rely on the insights of Polanyi with respect to the common framework of all economic activity, including the stock of trust and cooperation. And there can be no doubt that financialization played a central role in undermining that framework, even in those places, such as Greece, where it was relatively weak to begin with.

Social Inequalities

In the 1970s crisis, the dominant interpretation, which prepared the ground for the subsequent neoliberal settlement, was able to lay the blame on high wages, trade union power, the narrowing of inequality and consequently the weakening of market incentives, and the dependency culture created by the welfare state (Blyth, 2002). This was hardly likely to be convincing in the crisis of 2008. The years before the crisis were characterized by growing inequalities in income and wealth, the retreat of trade unions, falling labour shares and attempts to rein in the welfare state.

Harrison and Bluestone (1988) were amongst the first to document the 'great U-turn' in US income distribution, with falling inequality after the gilded age of the 1920s being reversed from the mid 1960s onwards. The same story was later taken up by Krugman (2002) in his account of the 'great compression', followed by the 'great divergence'.[52] Perhaps the single most astonishing statistic of all is given by Raghuram Rajan (2010): over a 30-year period (1976–2007), of every dollar of real income growth, 58 cents went to the top 1 per cent of households; a number subsequently turned into a slogan ('We are the 99 per cent') by the Occupy Wall Street movement.

Within mainstream economics, the emphasis in explaining these developments was placed on skill-biased technological change and the effects of trade.[53] As we have seen, the effects of trade liberalization, and the creation of a vast reserve army of labour on a global scale, put pressure on wages in both the developing and the developed world. Moreover, the threat of relocation, employed by firms in negotiations with their labour force, became more credible, even if it often included an element of bluff. And this threat was not only possible in so-called traditional industries, such as textiles or steel. By the 2000s, jobs in accounting or architectural offices, or in teaching and programming, could also be farmed out to the South, putting pressure on middle-class wages. The phenomenon of the 'indignados' and town-square protests, which we shall document in Chapter 5, was to some extent a middle-class phenomenon. From Cairo to Athens and Madrid, middle-class parents had been promised that they have little to fear from globalization, since their offspring could make social headway through education. But after gaining their Masters in Finance at City University or in Computing at Manchester, these young people often returned to working in their parents' store, or even to no job at all.

One of the ideological discourses of the period, repeated equally by Blairite social democrats or Bushite neo-conservatives, was the 'knowledge economy', as if previous periods in history had been based on ignorance. In 2006 Ben Bernanke, then newly appointed governor of the Fed, was taken to task by Paul Krugman in the *New York Times* for arguing that the most important factor behind the rise in inequality in the US was the skill premium – the increased return to education. As Krugman pointed out, the evidence for this particular thesis was thin: the earnings of graduates in the US had done only moderately well; from 1975 to 2004 the average earnings of college graduates rose, but less than 1 per cent a year.[54] Moreover, Hecker (1992) estimated that the proportion of college graduates over the age of 25 who were in 'non-college' jobs increased from 11 per cent in 1970 to 20 per cent in 1990.[55] Finally, McCormick, Horn and Knepper (1996) reported that the proportion of new college graduates claiming that their job did not require college-level skills increased continuously from 24 per cent in 1976 to 44 per cent in 1994. What these facts suggest is that capitalist development is in fact a very contradictory process, and that at the very time it needs new skills it also promotes deskilling of the workforce (Green, 2007).

The emphasis on trade and the skills premium leaves out considerations regarding institutional changes and developments at the top of the income, and wealth, distribution. The institutional environment was hostile to labour throughout the pre-crisis period almost everywhere. Anti-labour legislation was a common feature, as were measures to increase labour market 'flexibility'. Both Reagan and Thatcher strengthened their hand with symbolic victories over trade unions; against, respectively, air traffic control workers and the miners. Needless to say, but contrary to many neoliberal apologists, these victories against the 'insiders' led to no gains for the 'outsiders'. The growth of part-time, casual and precarious employment weakened workers, insiders and outsiders alike, and their ability to organize for better wages and working conditions. Here too, movements against precarious employment sprung up before the crisis, in countries such as France and Greece. That is not to say that the increasing levels of inequality and poverty stemmed only from the labour market. In the UK, for instance, a critical turn was the delinking of pensions from the growth of average earnings. Elsewhere it was the dismantling of central cornerstones of the welfare state, whether this was subsidies for children or the level of unemployment benefits.

Unemployment could, of course, be said to have played an independent contributing role. In the Golden Age, the commitment to full employment had evened things up between workers and employers in their bargaining over wages and conditions. The removal of that commitment, the replacement of growth with inflation targets, and the newly established 'independence' of central banks shifted the locus of power decisively in favour of employers.

At the other end of the distribution, where much of the action of increased inequality in income and wealth actually lies, institutional developments were also crucial. The drive to reduce the levels of taxation on the rich reached extravagant proportions in Bush's America, but it was a tendency to be found nearly everywhere. Corporation and income tax reductions were the order of the day, often packaged with the fanciful idea that the resulting effort from 'wealth creators' would lead to increases in tax revenues. This was also the period of tax havens and countless schemes invented to protect the riches of a small section of society. As Runciman (2011) argues, these schemes, tax law changes and other practices were introduced gradually and by stealth, thereby minimizing the opposition. Nor was it only a matter of formal institutions. Neoliberalism came packaged with a new individualistic ethic which legitimated greed, immortalized in Lord Mandelson's phrase that New Labour was 'intensely relaxed about people getting filthy rich'. The bonuses of the 'golden boys' of finance may have come into sharp focus after the crisis, with revulsion surpassing even that previously felt for corporate raiders and asset strippers, but there was little evidence of this before then. Thus changing social norms also have their place in the overall story.[56]

We have focused on the more liberal economies because not only did inequality increase the most, but this is where inequality developed into an independent causal factor in the crisis. The historic defeat of the working class associated with both Thatcherism and Reaganism transformed the balance of class forces to restore profits and increase the degree of labour exploitation. However, if median wages have been more or less stable since the 1970s (as in the US), but the average household keeps borrowing more and more, how can a crisis be avoided (Wolff, 2010)? Of course, incomes of households could be shored up in the short run, with more women entering the labour market and extending the number of hours worked, but there are clear limits to both processes (Konings and Panitch, 2008). The only option after a time was borrowing, and by 2007 the average American household had debt of more than 120 per cent of disposable income. Perry Anderson (2012: 55) describes this situation with his usual succinctness:

> the general implosion of the fictive capital with which markets throughout the developed world were kept going in the long cycle of financialization that began in the eighties, as profitability in the real economy contracted under the pressure of international competition, and rates of growth fell decade by decade. The mechanisms of this deceleration, internal to the workings of capital itself, will be familiar to any reader of Robert Brenner's work. In turn, its effects in the vast expansion of private and public debt, to prop up not only rates of profit but political electability, have been magisterially set out by Wolfgang Streeck ... The American economy illustrates this trajectory with paradigmatic clarity. But its logic has been system-wide.

This is the process that Colin Crouch (2009) was to name 'privatized keynesianism', with financial markets replacing (up to a point) the welfare state to shore up peoples' incomes. The object of the exercise was not primarily social, but to ensure enough demand and growth to keep the neoliberal show on the road. For in the period before the crisis it was generally accepted that the American consumer was the steam engine of world growth. The obvious conclusion was somehow not drawn by most commentators at the time: the neoliberal economy was not sufficiently dynamic, and having only partially dispensed with the prop of state Keynesianism, had to turn to another which, as we now know, would lead to devastating consequences.

Increased 'borrowing from the future' can be seen as a more general characteristic of capitalism since the late 1960s. For Streeck (2011a), the matter goes to the heart of the legitimacy of capitalism – to its ability to find a compromise with democracy. It was an issue that had been raised by Kalecki in 1943 in terms of whether capitalism was compatible with full employment. By the late 1960s, as the foundations of the post-war consensus began to crumble, both compatibilities were in serious doubt. In this context, borrowing (state as much as private) can be seen as an *endogenous* mechanism, postponing the final reckoning. 2008 was to provide, if not the final, a very serious reckoning.

Moreover, in this period of heightened inequalities we have seen that numerous movements sprang up to challenge the status quo. The movements against the financial system, as well as those of the precariat and the indignados, set the legitimacy of capitalism firmly on the agenda. They also brought to the fore the growing political crisis, a crisis of political representation, to which we now turn.

The Retreat of Democracy and the Crisis of Political Representation

We have argued that a progressive exit from the 1970s crisis would have entailed a deepening of the social-democratic settlement in the first two decades after World War II, enriching the existing institutions of political deliberation and economic democracy.[57]

Instead, the neoliberal turn sought to 'protect' the market from undue political influence and 'democratic overload'. What was needed was a recalibration of the political system to allow individuals to get on with their own lives without the heavy hand of the state or endless societal debate. The reality was rather different: a reconfiguration of power that provided elites with enhanced access to its corridors, while, at the same time, showing the exit to all those forms of collective action which sought redistribution and protection from market competition (Amable, 2010). Such a project needed action on many fronts.

One of these was the technocratic turn in economic policymaking. 'Independent' central banks constitute the paradigmatic case, even though the evidence for their supposed contribution to superior macroeconomic outcomes was always thin.[58] Their competence was to come into question even more starkly after the crisis, as we shall see presently with respect to the European Central Bank (ECB). Beyond the issue of competence, it was difficult to claim that central banks were independent from financial interests. Central bankers inhabited the same political and professional, not to mention social, environment as other financiers. Together they constituted an elite both 'in itself' and 'for itself'. Whenever the question arose, before or after the crisis, of who had to bear the cost for any necessary adjustment to the economy, financial interests were unlikely to top the list of potential candidates.

Many other regulatory authorities, especially in the newly privatized public utilities sector, sprung up like mushrooms in this period; part of the familiar process of deregulation followed by a hasty retreat necessitating re-regulation. But this re-regulation never returned things to the *status quo ante*. The regulators were faced with a huge asymmetry of resources and power; even if they were determined that regulation should mediate fairly between private and public interests.[59] Many were not. One of the most troubling aspects of all this was the way regulators were so often from the very industry being regulated, with a conflict of interest evident to all but the neoliberal governments that appointed them.[60]

Central and commercial bankers, businessmen, regulators, politicians and experts, with many of the latter funded by the interests involved, would meet in various settings as policymakers within their own nation state, or at the supranational level, to settle the main contours of policy. The undemocratic nature of this form of governance has already been broached in Chapter 1. Such networks, working groups and task forces were to be found not only in finance and business, but increasingly in the areas of health and education where the private sector was continually encroaching. And when the latter was not possible, private sector methods, quasi-markets and management techniques were more often than not the answer, whatever the problem in the remaining public sector (Hall, 2003).

Apart from the shifting values and priorities that this exercise incorporated, it usually implied a hollowing out of democracy

(Crouch, 2004), as existing deliberative and participatory institutions that had formerly been responsible for regulation and policy were either sidelined or closed down altogether. For all the talk of 'diversity', or 'care in the community', during this period there was a strengthening of central control (Pollock, 2005). Not surprisingly, this led to a widespread feeling of loss of control for citizens who felt they had no say in the running of their hospitals or schools.

Not that this sense of control was any more secure at the central level. For the result of the convergence of the centre-left and centre-right parties in this period, and the rise of the cartel party phenomenon discussed in Chapter 1, was that general elections did not seem to matter as much as before. It was often difficult to claim that voters were presented with a real choice, especially where economic policy was concerned. And even when they were, this was often negated in the policies of the government after the election. Centrist analysts were likely to blame structure over agency for this sad state of affairs, pointing their finger at the structural constraints that constricted all governments in the more globalized era, as well as the enhanced power of supranational organizations such as the IMF and the WTO. But as we have seen, these resulted from concrete policy and institutional interventions; and what is more, ones which the parties of the centre-left, as much as those of the centre-right, were likely to have supported.

The first result of all these tendencies was the widespread alienation from politics and declining levels of political participation. As Marquand (2004) pithily puts it: if nobody listens what is the point of debate? For Marquand, this is the context in which to see the 'return to the politics of connection, favouritism and patronage' – as other values, such as public service and political participation, have been sidelined, the distinction between legal, 'dodgy but not quite illegal', and illegal transactions between self-interested individuals has become increasingly fuzzy. Thus the rise of corruption, also discussed at some length in Chapter 1, is a second consequence of the retreat of democracy. A third is the growth of far-right political forces, from the Tea Party in the US, to the National Front in France and Golden Dawn in Greece. There are large differences in political content and practice within these examples, but to some extent they all reflect a certain frustration with traditional politics, and a feeling that existing parties do not represent the interests of many sections of society (Frank, 2006). The other side of the same coin is the crisis of representation faced by all mainstream political parties, but more acutely those of the centre-left; not only because of their history and the nature of their traditional social base, but also because they lack ready-made alternative discourses of the patriotic or cultural variety.

The retreat of democracy and the crisis of political representation have a more direct role in the story running up to the crisis and how it was dealt with afterwards. Both phenomena are characteristic of a growing distance between ruling elites and ordinary people. Increasingly, the former were unaware or indifferent to the plight of the latter, and this could not help but have a bearing on the policies pursued. Finally, the two phenomena allowed the various forms of resistance to the policies pursued after the crisis to appropriate the democratic mantle, which is an important development – as we shall see in the final two chapters of the book.

2008

The final eruption of the crisis can be succinctly summarized, as there are numerous detailed accounts available on all the various facets involved. The first indication that something was seriously afoot was the credit squeeze that materialized by 2007. At the same time, the real-estate boom in the US was going into reverse, which brought into sharper focus the origins of some of the toxic financial instruments that had seen phenomenal growth in the preceding period. In March of the following year Bear Stearns effectively went bankrupt and had to be rescued by J P Morgan Chase. And of course, the whole thing imploded in September when Lehman Brothers were allowed to fail.[61]

The strictly financial aspects of the crisis are also rather well understood.[62] Our own analysis here relies heavily on Minsky's work on financial crises (Laskos and Tsakalotos, 2011: 95–104), and in particular his insight that financial markets are particularly susceptible to too much competition, leading to excessive risk taking. Most financial crises[63] start with some innovation suggesting that risk can be borne or distributed more effectively, and that financial lending can expand on a surer footing. The hope engendered is always that 'this time is different', as suggested by the very title of Reinhart and Rogoff's (2009) mainstream, but perceptive, account.

In the third world debt crisis of the 1970s, the innovation was the lending to states by a consortium of banks. This time around it was the process of securitization which lay behind so many of the toxic financial instruments. Competitive pressures ensured the familiar cycle in which more and more competitors join the business, profit margins fall, more risky loans are made, and in the end speculative activity begins to take off, all in the hope of keeping profits rising steadily (Minsky, 1982). In the latest episode in the US, things began to unravel after the collapse of the housing market brought into question the ultimate source of the toxic loans. Banks began to worry about whether these loans would ever be repaid, and thus about the quality of the financial assets held by other banks. It took the Lehman Brothers collapse to turn the credit crunch into a financial crisis.

The above provides no more than a barebones account of the financial crisis. The emphasis of this chapter has been on the larger picture, and what Hall and Massey (2010) have called the 'many moments' of the crisis.[64] Our account of the five interdependent processes behind the crisis are intended to shed light on these moments. Thus, to understand why so much finance was available to fund the housing and derivatives bubble, one has to understand the macroeconomic imbalances that resulted from the process of globalization, and which have been so astutely analysed by Yiannis Varoufakis (2011). Schematically, low Chinese wages allowed for highly competitive goods to be exported to the US. The consequent current account deficit of the US was financed by Chinese investments, providing both the funds, and ensuring low interest rates, to keep inflating the bubble. Before 2008, prestigious American economists could claim that the US current account deficit was of no concern because it was covered by quality financial assets, but the situation was clearly unsustainable.

What we could refer to as the social moment also comes into play here. The toxic assets had their origin in loans to some of the poorer sections of American society (Konings and Panitch, 2008); loans that would have hardly been necessary had real wages fared better in the preceding period. Nor would they have been necessary if the political process in the US was open to working people in order for them to be able to put, say, investment in public social housing onto the political agenda. Privatized Keynesianism, just like the previous state variety, seems to have very real limits.

The ideological moment also plays a prominent role. Neoliberalism had legitimized greed among the financiers, who were quite happy to take increasing risks not only with their customers' money, but also with that of their own financial institution. Individualism, credit-reliance and consumerism fuelled the various bubbles – financial and housing – while also providing ideological cover not only for the 'excesses', but for the essence of the underlying economic model. People were not supposed to be fulfilled as citizens, but as consumers who could 'vote' every day of every year through their purchases.[65] Public deliberation on, say, the role of the stock market and the financial system in a modern society, was not part of the neoliberal order – these could be left to the individual and decentralized decision of millions of people acting on their own self-interest.

But we can also look at these various moments through time. This has been done by Harvey (2010), who has argued that the form capitalist crises take undergoes a transformation as the economic, but also political, response to one crisis leads to the reappearance of underlying problems in some other guise. Thus (simplifying greatly with respect to the richness of his analysis) neoliberalism can be seen as a response to the overaccumulation crisis of the late 1960s. But this led to a latent crisis of underconsumption, as wages and state spending stagnated, which was met with loans to wider sections of the population. This in turn led to the financial crisis. Our own account of the multiple processes that accompanied the period before the financial crisis, we hope, elucidates some of the forces behind the shifting trajectory of capitalist crises.

Whatever the underlying causes of the 2008 crisis, there are a number of proximate causes that are highlighted even by the more enlightened analysts of mainstream thinking such as Raghuram Rajan (2010). Three of the most prominent of these are: macroeconomic imbalances, the level of social inequality and the regulation of the banks. None of these three were of central concern to ruling elites after 2008. And the EU's response, to which we now turn, was particularly problematic in this respect.

CRISIS IN THE EUROZONE

[W]hereas in the US, massive public bail-outs could stave off the collapse of insolvent banks, insurance companies and corporations, and the printing of money by the Federal Reserve could check contraction of demand, two barriers blocked any such temporary resolution in the Eurozone. There, not only did the Statutes of the ECB, enshrined in the Treaty of Maastricht, expressively forbid it from buying the debt of member states, but there was no *Schicksalgemeinschaft* – that 'community of fate' of the Weberian nation – to bind rulers and ruled together in a common political order, in which the former will pay a heavy price for ignoring altogether the existential needs of the latter.

In the European simulacrum of federalism, there could be no 'transfer union' along American lines. Once crisis struck, cohesion in the Eurozone could only come, not from social expenditure, but political dictation – the enforcement by Germany, at the head of a block of small northern states, of draconian austerity programmes, unthinkable for its own citizens, on the southern periphery, no longer able to recover competitively by devaluation. Anderson (2012: 56–7)

In the US and the Eurozone, for both governments and central banks, the response to the crisis was of a similar order but of a different intensity. The immediate concern, not unjustifiably, was to bail out the financial system, and to prevent contagion leading once more to a great depression. There was a determination not to repeat the mistakes of 1929, but initially it remained a grey area as to whether this would entail going beyond salvaging the banks. For a while after the Lehman debacle, a more radical agenda seemed to be in the offing, with not only the banks but many of the other pillars of the neoliberal order being subjected to public criticism, not to say derision. But the moment passed, ruling elites breathed a sigh of relief, and got down to the job of damage-limitation and recovering the thread of pre-crisis policy.

Having said that, the US government and the Fed, in terms of the fiscal and monetary stimulus offered, was far more activist than anything the Eurozone could match. Prominent commentators, such as Paul Krugman in his biweekly column in the *New York Times,* would argue that the new Obama administration, which took over in January 2009, was not doing enough and that it was vital not stop either stimuli too early. But both he, as well as commentators across the Atlantic, such as Martin Wolf[66] and Wolfgang Munchau writing in the *Financial Times,* were convinced that compared to the Americans, the Europeans were not doing anything like enough to prevent a worsening of the Eurozone crisis. Other articles on the ignorance of basic economics, foot-dragging and the general incompetence of European leaders were a regular feature in the following years (Eijffinger, 2009). The charge of being constantly 'behind the curve' was an oft-repeated theme here.

However, in much of the European press, and not only that of Germany, another angle was developing that put the Eurozone crisis in a different perspective. Especially after the Greek crisis started in earnest in 2010, a narrative formed, which in many respects mirrored that of the dominant one within Greece, in which a productive and efficient North had to bail out a South that was determined to keep its more consumer-orientated and leisurely lifestyle. The reforms necessary for challenging this state of affairs had not gone far enough – they never do in neoliberal accounts – and thus the crisis must be used to complete the reform agenda.

This helped to keep the focus on government debt. Critics would rail that, with the possible exception of Greece,[67] the fiscal crisis was a result of the financial crisis, the salvaging of the banks, and not its cause. In this context, the austerity measures that came to dominate Eurozone policymaking, and indeed politics, were misplaced. But such criticism fell on deaf ears, and as a result two seemingly inexorable vicious circles began. The first saw the financial crisis transforming itself into a fiscal crisis, which led to further financial instability: since banks held considerable amounts of government bonds, they required more state aid. The second was the way austerity measures led to greater-than-expected recession, with the result that yet more measures had to be implemented. The timeline in the Appendix amply demonstrates how these two cycles fed off each other and how European leaders had to continuously deal with both, to little avail.

This ineffectual response of Eurozone leaders to the crisis needs more careful attention. We will run with two possible hypotheses. The first we call the *structural incompetence hypothesis*. This suggests that the inadequate response was due to the structural limits imposed by the inherited economic and financial architecture of the Eurozone; limits which poor leadership, the existence of the type of cognitive locking discussed in the Introduction, or simply the incompetence of European leaders was unable to overcome. The second can be thought of as the *class instinct hypothesis*. This suggest a more wily leadership, aware that it must play for time if the neoliberal agenda is to be renewed after the crisis, and if the burden of the debt is to be placed on those classes least responsible for its creation. Merkel's vision of a conservative federation, to be enshrined wherever possible in the constitution of the EU, could be seen as evidence for the second hypothesis. After all, it is a vision which seems to encompass many of the elements of our previous analysis in this chapter: restricted democracy; unrestricted inequality in the periphery of the Eurozone as a source of cheap labour; and technocratic governance, with the financial system hardly having to change gear from its previous practices.

It remains to be seen whether these two hypotheses can be combined into a coherent account, and to what extent the policies pursued in the period were in any sense rational.

Architectural Origins of the Eurozone

Since the beginning of the European integration process, two interrelated processes have predominated. The first is the priority given to negative, as opposed to positive, integration. The second is that economics, and not politics, has been in the driving seat.

Negative integration entails removing obstacles to the free movement of goods, services, labour and capital. The explicit contradistinction is with positive integration, the process of building new institutions to replace powers and institutions given up by member states in order to make integration work better. The advanced pace of integration that was initiated in 1986 with the Single European Act was very much in the negative mode. The defeat of the Alternative Economic Strategy in Britain in the 1970s and the retreat from the Common Programme of the Left in France in 1983 are, in retrospect, highly significant signposts of what was to come.

These reversals underlined the failure of any Left exit from the crisis of the 1970s, and ensured that the integration process would be under the hegemony of the Right, Delors' rearguard interventions with respect to Social Europe notwithstanding. By the mid-1990s, the negative integration bias was given an added boost by the gradual incorporation into the EU of the economies of Eastern Europe and the Balkans. The widening, rather than deepening, agenda looked to a union as a vast 'free' market for entrepreneurship and competition. Its strongest advocates were British Conservatives, from Thatcher to Cameron, and New Labour under Blair. In both cases the class instinct hypothesis seems particularly germane.

The Monnet method of placing economics in command of the integration process may have been instigated well before the neoliberal era, but it fitted in nicely with the priorities of the later period. The original conception, often associated with neofunctionalist analysis, seems to have been that as one phase of economic integration would give rise to the necessity of the next, European peoples would become more integrated almost by stealth (Tsakatika, 2007). They would then naturally take the next step to form themselves into a European people demanding that the democratic deficit be corrected. It did not seem to occur to the visionaries of European integration that this path would lead to a particular configuration of power that would be seen as an additional bonus to the elites that benefitted most, rather than as a further obstacle to be overcome on the way to a more democratic United States of Europe. The European-wide version of the democratic deficit,[68] the lack of a European people as well as a particularly impenetrable form of political governance, were unable to prevent the crisis, and more importantly still, were singularly inadequate material for responding to the crisis once it broke out. This way of looking at things combines elements from both the class instinct and structural incompetence hypotheses.

Negative integration and the democratic deficit constituted the background conditions, not only for the Single European Act, but also for all further integrative drives, notably European employment policies, and of course, monetary union itself. The results in terms of growth, employment and unemployment were well below expectations. The dynamic boost to growth expected from the single market never materialized. The European employment policy, based on the principles of adaptability, employability and entrepreneurship, was neoliberal in intent with a few neo-Keynesian touches to keep up appearances. But, in terms of outcomes, it fared no better than the single market.[69] This leaves monetary union and the creation of the Eurozone, to which we now turn.

Macroeconomic Imbalances of the Eurozone

In Chapter 2 we saw that in the period before the crisis, in terms of per capita income, Greece had been able to converge on European levels to a great extent. The same goes for the other countries of the periphery, later to be grouped together as the PIGS (with the 'I' referring to Ireland and sometimes Italy as well). But this was also a period of large divergences with respect to both current accounts and inflation rates.

Figure 3.2 shows current account positions as a percentage of GDP in 1999, 2007 and 2008.[70] It illustrates that since the formation of the euro area there has been a tendency to divergence. Greece is not alone in experiencing a growing deficit – this was also true of Portugal, Spain and Malta. At the same time, countries such as Germany and the Netherlands had significant, persistent and growing surpluses. Effectively, what we have here is a regional version of the global imbalances between the US and Asia.

What lies behind these persistent and worsening imbalances? Germany, as a country not generating internal demand, had low price (and indeed wage) inflation. The Southern countries, as countries generating internal demand, have had higher price (wage) inflation. Figure 3.3 shows the differential between individual

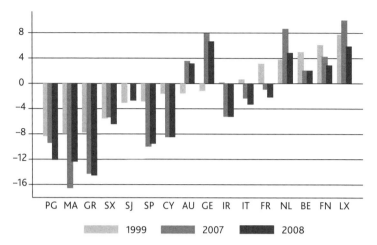

Figure 3.2   Euro area countries: current account as % of GDP

Source: Eurostat – National accounts and General Government data.

countries' inflation and that of the euro area average in each year from 1999 to 2011. We can note the consistently positive inflation differential in the PIGS and compare that to the consistently negative inflation differential in Germany. Given the low level of inflation in the euro area in general, it is quite impressive for a country to have had inflation below the average in every year.

Figure 3.4 underlies the strong competitive position of the German, and coincidentally Swedish, economy. But Figure 3.5 is even more revealing in that it shows that the growing divergence in competiveness was not related to any lack of productivity increases in the South. In Greece productivity increases actually outstripped those of Germany, especially in the later period. Rather, it is the German restrictive wages policy after 2000 that made it almost impossible for the periphery to compete (Lapavitsas et al., 2010). So whoever the beneficiaries of existing arrangements were, it was not the workers of Germany and more generally the North.

From this we can deduce that any narrative on a productive North having to bail out a more leisurely South is misleading. It also hides the real winners from the whole process. German economic success before 2008 depended on exporting, not least to the South. It thus benefited from the demand generated by the PIGS; the other side of the coin of Southern deficits was Northern surpluses. In 2007, German net exports of goods to the PIGS (goods exported by Germany to the PIGS minus goods imported by Germany from the

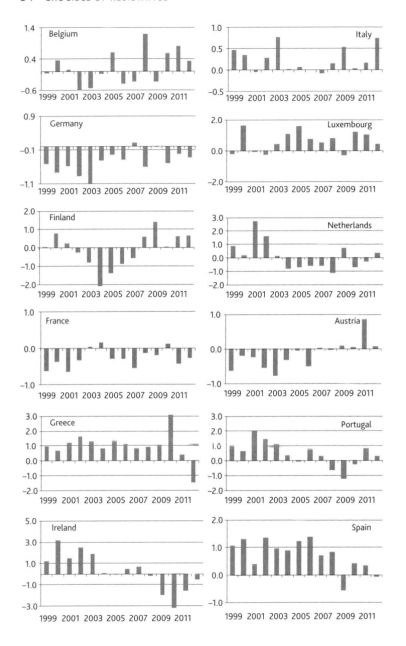

Figure 3.3   Deviation of national inflation rates from euro area inflation rates

Source: Authors' calculations from EUROSTAT.

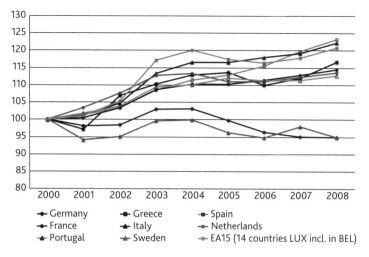

Figure 3.4   Relative nominal unit labour costs (2000 = 100)

Source: AMECO Database.

Notes: Nominal unit labour cost for each country is the ratio of compensation per employee to real GDP per person employed. It is expressed in US dollars and calculated relative to the rest of the 35 industrial countries (EU 27, with Luxembourg included in Belgium, plus Turkey, Norway, Switzerland, the US, Japan, Canada, Mexico, Australia and New Zealand) using double export weights.

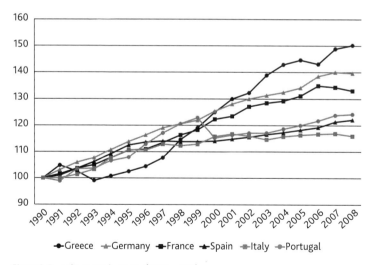

Figure 3.5   Labour productivity (1990 = 100)

Source: Total Economy Database (The Conference Board, 2011) (http://www.conference-board.org/data/economydatabase/ – accessed May 2013); authors' calculations.

Notes: Labour productivity is measured as real GDP per hour worked. Real GDP is expressed in 1990 US$ (converted at Geary–Khamis PPPs).

PIGS) were equivalent to 1.43 per cent of German GDP (see Table 3.2). This represented over 17 per cent of Germany's trade account surplus (fourth column). If we include Italy, the evidence becomes stronger. The net trade in goods between Germany and the PI(I)GS amounted to some 2.24 per cent of GDP in 2007 (fifth column), accounting for 27.5 per cent of Germany's trade account surplus.

In general, Germany depends quite heavily on demand generated within the rest of the European Union. In 2007, when the trade account was 8.15 per cent of GDP, some 4.44 per cent of GDP (i.e. 63.4 per cent of the trade account surplus) originated in Germany's surplus arising from its export of goods to other EU countries over its imports from EU countries. So if Greece and the other PIGS had not been growing during this period, Germany's growth would not have been as healthy.

But German, and in general Northern, gains do not only rest here. The credit dependence that Germany had proudly avoided at home was effectively exported abroad (Rajan, 2010). Current account deficits have to be financed, and Northern banks were more than willing to fulfil the role. Indeed, they did this with enthusiasm. There is an argument to be had about the direction of causation of these flows. For it could be argued that the high profitability of economies such as Greece attracted an inflow of funds, in which case the current account deficit is more a consequence than cause. But whatever is the case, it cannot be doubted that German exporters and financiers were one of the chief beneficiaries of existing Eurozone arrangements.

Post-Crisis

The main directions of the Eurozone response to the crisis were established by the end of 2010. These were: austerity, perseverance with the neoliberal reform programme, and step-by-step approaches to problems as they arose. For European leaders there were transitional costs to be borne, not primarily because of the profligacy of banks, but because so many nation states had not played by the rulebook before the crisis. The latter needed more transparent and binding rules embedded in the constitution. Moreover, politicians were increasingly seen as inherently untrustworthy trustees of these rules, especially in the South.

The support given to Mario Monti in Italy, and Lucas Papademos in Greece, gave a new twist to the technocratic spirit of the whole enterprise. Eurozone priorities, policies and institutional interventions were first agreed between Angela Merkel and Nicolas

Table 3.2 Importance of PIGS in German trade

	German current account (% GDP)	German trade account (% GDP)	German trade with PIGS (% of German GDP)	Percentage of German trade account surplus originating in trade with PIGS	German trade with PIIGS (% of German GDP)	Percentage of German trade account surplus originating in trade with PIIGS
1999	−1.26	3.21	0.29	9.00	0.54	16.96
2000	−1.70	2.92	0.31	10.46	0.74	25.32
2001	0.02	4.62	0.22	4.66	0.78	16.83
2002	2.04	6.23	0.46	7.39	1.11	17.81
2003	1.92	5.93	0.51	8.65	1.21	20.37
2004	4.66	6.78	0.71	10.54	1.51	22.24
2005	5.12	6.93	0.90	12.95	1.74	25.05
2006	6.52	6.78	1.19	17.58	1.96	28.92
2007	7.92	8.15	1.43	17.52	2.24	27.46
2008	6.69	7.31	1.21	16.60	1.81	24.82

Source: IMF, International Financial Statistics and Direction of Trade Statistics.

Sarkozy, the latter to be replaced later by Françoise Hollande, before being put to lesser European leaders for the ensuing 'tough' negotiating process. In this light the term democratic deficit hardly seems adequate. The timeline in the Appendix charts all these phenomena in some detail. In short, the problem was not neoliberalism, but an insufficient commitment to its tenets – one can almost hear the echoes of some diehard supporters of the East European regimes in the years before their collapse.

The structural incompetence hypothesis is lent support by the existence of cognitive locking and the lack of a thinking capacity in Eurozone institutions. Perry Anderson has spoken of European 'narcissism' in these years. The economic and financial architecture of the EU did not seem to incorporate any insights concerning the basic economic principles of monetary union, even though this could have been gleaned from even a cursory reading of Paul De Grawe's textbook on the *Economics of Monetary Union*, taught in almost every economics department of every member state of the EU.

It seemed beyond the architects of monetary union to recognize: that monetary unions need a proper central bank to act as a lender of last resort, to both member states and banks; that they must have some institutions to provide automatic stabilizers and offer a degree of solidarity to areas in crisis; that the macroeconomic policy of the union must be undertaken with respect to macroeconomic conditions prevailing throughout the union and not just those of the North; and that Germany cannot act as a small open economy, indifferent to the level of demand in the union as a whole. It is dangerous to become a hostage to your own rhetoric – having believed that neoliberal integration would lead to dynamic growth and prevent future capitalist crises, no provision was made for the eventuality that such sanguine conclusions would be disproved.

Nor was there any evidence of any greater familiarity with the economics of recession, and the way such recessions can become self-propagating. The existence of the debt trap, when one tries to reduce debt as a percentage of GDP by cutting expenditure with the result that income falls at a faster rate than does debt, seemed to be a *terra incognita* in official policy circles. The fact that debt levels increased throughout the Eurozone in the years after 2008 did not seem to provide food for thought for European leaders – confirmation of the basic Kuhnian maxim that empirical evidence on its own is rarely sufficient to change the ruling paradigm of thought. There were many more instances of European leaders seemingly in denial. One could mention the early upbeat announcements of prospects for a quick recovery; or the insistence that Greece only faced a liquidity and not an insolvency problem. When, in turn, this became untenable it was replaced by the determination that no other nation state would need a bailout.

More serious still, Eurozone institutions did not seem to have the thinking capacity to react to the crisis once it appeared. Decision making was tortuous and subject to multiple delays. It also lacked popular legitimacy. In the vacuum created, the ECB started filling in some of the blanks. In the early period of the crisis the ECB had failed to understand the seriousness of the situation, worrying about the danger of future rises in inflation as, one might add, Rome was burning. More important still, because it failed to act as a lender of last resort, indebted states faced a liquidity risk that increased the cost of borrowing and actually deepened the debt crisis.[71] But slowly it started to circumvent its own, and the EU's, constitution by buying up the government bonds of distressed nations in the secondary markets and offering enhanced liquidity to the financial system. By the summer of 2012 Mario Draghi, the president of the ECB, was promising to do whatever it took in order to avoid the collapse of the Eurozone, whether through supporting banks or sovereign bonds. While Draghi was committed to the whole panoply of neoliberal reforms, he was fully aware of the threats to the system. Moreover, he insisted that despite the actions the ECB could take, it could not provide an overall resolution to the Eurozone crisis. That had to be a matter for the political leaders of the union.

But an overall solution was what European leaders, and especially the Germans, resisted: as the timeline demonstrates, one European Council, or Eurogroup, meeting after another spectacularly failed to come up with a coherent overall response. Angela Merkel and her finance minister, Wolfgang Schäuble, were apt to point to the moral hazard of any overall solution to the debt problem. In other words, any solution including, for instance, a European-wide investment drive, would alleviate the pressure on nation states to carry out the necessary reforms. This seems to give greater credence to the class instinct hypothesis – that the lack of an overall solution was part of a strategy to impose a more rigorous neoliberal order and/or a more authoritarian conception of federalism.

The unswaying commitment to austerity and the neoliberal reform programme also gives support to the class instinct hypothesis. But what of the level of rationality implied by this hypothesis? If we attribute to European leaders a greater level of strategic thinking, did they foresee the level of recession that resulted from the policies of austerity, and not only in the South? Had they factored into their calculations the extent of the backlash to these policies and the danger of a renaissance of ultra-right-wing or secessionist forces; or for that matter, the size of the opposition from more progressive forces (to be discussed in the last two chapters)?

Harvey's (2010) analysis of the shifting forms of capitalist crises suggests that a strategy for sorting out one facet of a crisis can eventually lead it (or another facet) emerging in another form. This alerts us to the fact that a capitalist crisis has systemic features that may not be amenable to treatment, even with the most rational of actors. For instance, if the Merkel/Schäuble strategy implied that some central features of monetary unions, such as a large federal budget or a normal central bank with the powers of the Fed, would be instigated only after the forces of labour had been defeated, then what is the guarantee that German voters, imbued with the narrative of lazy Southerners, would accept a solution entailing far greater levels of social solidarity across Europe when the time came?

On its own the structural incompetence hypothesis fails to convince. On the one hand, there was a great deal of continuity in policy orientation before and after the crisis. This cannot merely be put down to inertia or path dependency. On the other, after 2010 there was a good deal of informational feedback about the dire consequences of the selected approach, and, as we have seen, plenty of criticism available even from within elite circles.[72] Alternative paths were available, but what we witnessed instead was the lack of plasticity in the system that was broached in the Introduction of this book. That lack is still in need of a convincing explanation.

This suggests that the class instinct hypothesis is worth pursuing – even if our comments on the rationality of the elite response, and the existence of systemic features beyond the influence of individual agents, point to the need to incorporate insights from both hypotheses. The next two chapters of the book will shed some more light on some of the questions just posed.

4
From Crisis to Permanent Austerity

> Then, behind the Government, is a small mercantile and banking cabal. This cabal is determined above all to protect its financial prerogatives, at whatever expense to the economic health of the country. Its members wish to retain a tax system rigged fantastically in their favor. They oppose exchange controls, because these might prevent them from salting away their profits in banks in Cairo or Argentina. They would never dream of investing these profits in their country's recovery. Porter (1947: 106)[73]

Throughout most of 2009 Prime Minister Kostas Karamanlis was prone to boast about how much his administration had sheltered the Greek economy from the ongoing world economic crisis, and how little the Greek banking system was exposed to the toxic financial products that had wreaked so much havoc elsewhere. But in the run-up to the October election he was striking a more cautious note: whatever government emerged would have to take tough measures to stabilize the economy. The PASOK opposition, under George Papandreou, in an attempt to differentiate itself not only from the New Democracy government but also from the previous PASOK administrations of Kostas Simitis, adopted a more Keynesian stance, claiming that 'money was available' for a more expansionary policy and promising real wage increases 'whatever the level of the deficit'.[74] There was nothing before the autumn of that year to remotely prepare the Greek people for what was to come.

What becomes very clear from even a cursory examination of the timeline of the Greek crisis (see Appendix) is the speed and remorselessness of events that followed the formation of the new PASOK administration. After a brief period of 'phoney war', in which the key feature was political wrangling between the new PASOK government and the opposition about the size of, and responsibility for, the public sector deficit, it became clear that something was seriously wrong beyond the integrity of 'Greek statistics'. Greeks became increasingly familiar with the significance of interest rate spreads, credit agencies and 'credit watch negative'. The worsening financial situation, and doubts about the future ability of the government to borrow on the open markets, were constantly affected by new information about the real size of the deficit, the extent of government arrears (for instance to pharmaceutical companies) and contagion effects from elsewhere.[75]

By May 2010 the Eurozone countries, and the IMF, had agreed a €110 billion package for Greece in return for a standard IMF structural adjustment programme, including a huge fiscal consolidation, to be 'monitored' by the so-called Troika representing the interests of Greece's creditors (EU-ECB-IMF). A second adjustment package followed in July of 2011. Parliament was confronted with a continuous stream of budgets, new austerity measures, medium-term fiscal strategies (MTFS) and omnibus bills including 'prior actions' (necessary for financing to continue), Financing was paid out in tranches; disbursements were often delayed and nearly always preceded by political turmoil as pressure was exerted by the Troika to ensure compliance.[76]

Politics, not surprisingly, was also in fast-forward mode. The Papandreou government, under the pressure of popular mobilization, had to give way to that of Lucas Papademos in November 2011. Papademos, a former governor of the Bank of Greece and vice-president of the ECB was a favourite of both the Troika and important business and media interests within Greece itself. The media, in particular, prepared the ground for a prime minister from outside the established political system.

Papademos was chosen for his technocratic prowess and his affinity with financial markets. But he proved a far inferior political operator compared to Mario Monti in Italy;[77] although, to be fair, the support offered from PASOK was only partial and that from New Democracy even more equivocal. As a result, the government only lasted until the spring of 2012. The double elections (May and July) led to the third successive pro-austerity government; this time under Antonis Samaras, leader of New Democracy, but with the active support of both PASOK and the Democratic Left.[78] At the same time the rise of SYRIZA, as the main party of opposition, signalled a new phase in the political conflict. For the first time a pro-austerity government faced an opposition that wanted to reject the whole logic of the economic policies pursued since May 2010.[79]

Throughout this period, the Greek establishment – technocratic and intellectual as much as political – seemed to be in denial. It was in good company – it was Jürgen Stark, at the time a member of the ECB executive board, who had pronounced in January 2010 that the EU would not bail Greece out. At first it was claimed that Greece did not need any adjustment programme. After May 2010 it was continuously stressed, by technocrats such as Lucas Papademos and Giannis Stournaras (the future minister of finance in the Samaras government), that any restructuring of the debt, a haircut as it became to be known, would prove disastrous. For Evangelos Venizelos, minister of finance in the Papademos government and leader of PASOK after the fall of George Papandreou, restructuring was cheap, almost unpatriotic, talk. However, after the debt swap in February 2012, and the buyback in December of the same year, the same people would claim that restructuring was in fact a central plank of the strategy of national salvation and a great success.[80]

But celebrations for such 'successes' were usually short-lived. A distinct pattern was apparent from the first stages of the crisis, for Greece as for the rest of the Eurozone: a new solution would be announced, and markets and spreads would react favourably only to be followed by a period of uncertainty as it became clear that the solution was far from complete. It was the unsustainability of the debt that frequently underpinned such uncertainty. The IMF continuously had to revise its forecast for the future course of Greek debt, as can be seen from Figure 4.1.

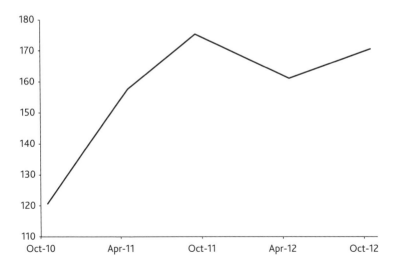

Figure 4.1   IMF projections for the Greek debt-to-GDP ratio in 2012 at various dates

Source: Calculated from World Economic Outlook data (IMF, October 2010, April 2011, September 2011, April 2012 and October 2012).

Part of the problem was the unrealistic nature of the adjustment programmes themselves. By the time of the debt swap in February 2012, which cut a net amount of 20 percentage points[81] from the Greek debt-to-GDP ratio, the IMF was forecasting that the ratio would reach a sustainable level of 120 per cent by 2020. Apart from the fact that this target seemed arbitrary – reflecting merely the Italian level that was assumed to be sustainable – the forecast was unrealistic: in the years running up to 2020, primary (general) government surpluses would be of the order of 4.5 per cent, while, at the same time, growth would be about 3 per cent per year. The inclusion of €50 billion worth of revenues from privatization only served to stretch the level of incredulity to breaking point. Meanwhile, the IMF was constantly revising its forecasts for growth in the Eurozone downwards, and similar austerity programmes were being pursued elsewhere (see Table 4.1).

Table 4.1   IMF forecasts for GDP growth in 2012 (%)

	January 2011	September 2011	January 2012	July 2012	October 2012
World GDP	4.5	4.0	3.3	3.5	3.3
Euro area	1.7	1.1	−0.5	−0.3	−0.4
USA	2.7	1.8	1.8	2.0	2.2

Source: IMF Economic Outlook (various issues).

However, for elites within and beyond Greece the commitment to austerity never wavered. The initial fiscal consolidation envisaged in May 2010 was for the general government deficit to be reduced from 13.6 per cent of GDP to 3 per cent by 2014. While the government promised a speedy return to growth, its absence sealed Greece's entry into a debt trap; and a vicious circle where austerity policies led to a greater-than-predicted recession, with a consequent failure to meet revenue and expenditure targets and the imposition of a new round of austerity. While one prime minister, or one minister of finance, after another would pledge that a particular austerity package would be the last, this was quickly negated in practice. The constant expectation of more measures had economic consequences, as agents factored them in to their consumption and investment decisions. But the political impact was, if anything, even greater for the credibility of the political establishment.

We return to the social and political opposition to austerity in Chapter 5. For the moment we turn to some critical questions. Why was it Greece that led the dance of the Eurozone crisis, and was the imposition of a structural adjustment package under the Troika's control an unavoidable outcome?

WHY GREECE?

Financial crises are often difficult to predict. They may even have an element of inherent unpredictability. Thus, the orthodox literature on the subject has moved some distance from first-generation models that claimed such crises stem from problems with fundamentals, such as excessive inflation or public sector deficits.[82] Second-generation models were developed in response to the ERM crises of 1992 and 1993.[83] In these models, pegging the exchange rate to reduce inflation becomes increasingly untenable because it is associated with ever more unemployment, ever higher interest rates and increasing financial distress. Speculators recognizing the policy dilemmas can spark off a crisis that ultimately becomes self-fulfilling – the government has to abandon the peg because of the economic cost. Finally, third-generation models move even further away from fundamentals and, moreover, are not confined to currency crises. De Grauwe (2012) uses such a model to explain the Eurozone sovereign debt crisis. The mere fear of a sovereign default in the Eurozone causes bond yields to rise and generates a liquidity crisis for the government which actually provokes the default, as the government is either unable to refinance its debt (at any level of interest rate) or can only do so at such a high level that the debt dynamics rapidly deteriorate.[84]

From our own perspective, the systemic nature of the crisis also allows for a degree of randomness as to the initial breaking point. But randomness can take us only so far. Greece, as we have argued, was exposed to many of the 'moments' of the crisis – the social and democratic deficits were particularly acute – while exhibiting many of the strengths and weaknesses of a neoliberal economy. In the dominant narrative in Greece, on the other hand, the problem lay in the absence of structural reforms and the malign influence of populism: whatever the cause of the crisis elsewhere, it was fiscal irresponsibility which ensured that Greece would be the most vulnerable Eurozone economy.

From Figure 4.2 we can see that a high level of debt, around 100 per cent of GDP, was a feature of the economy from the early

1990s.[85] The same can be said of the deficit, although there is a clear worsening after 2007.[86] Unlike Spain and Portugal, however, Greece had a far smaller private sector debt problem, and its commercial banks were far less exposed to the financial crisis than was the case in Spain, Ireland or Cyprus, not to mention France and Germany. So, on balance, it is not clear that someone in 2008 could have predicted that Greece would become the weak link. And from the fact that such predictions were not frequent has political relevance for the story we are telling.

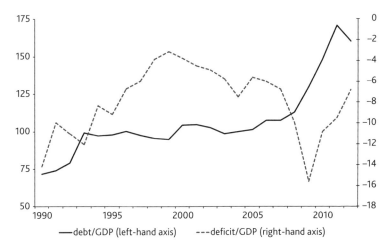

Figure 4.2 General government debt/GDP and deficit/GDP ratios (% of GDP)

Source: Eurostat – National accounts and General Government data.

To understand Greece's vulnerability we need to look at what lies behind the deficits and the debt. As we saw in Chapter 1, the size of the Greek public sector is much exaggerated in the dominant narrative. And as we can see from Figures 4.3 and 4.4, the divergence from EU levels stems much more from the revenue than the expenditure side.

What lies behind this revenues deficit? We have already addressed the role of falling tax rates, especially on profits, in the modernizing programme in the years before 2008. Between 2004 and 2008, while taxable profits increased by about 35 per cent, revenues from private sector firms actually fell by 2 per cent. Another major contributing factor was tax evasion. Thus Stathakis (2010) reports that Greece's 900,000 private firms contributed only about 4 per cent of total tax revenues. The owners of small shops and the self-employed, from plumbers to private sector doctors, rarely provided their customers with receipts. Moreover, if we are to believe income tax receipts, Greece is bereft of rich citizens, as only a tiny percentage of the population declare incomes above €50,000. It would not be an exaggeration to say that a large section of the population pays taxes on a voluntary basis, leaving wage-earners, who cannot hide their incomes, to pick up the tab.

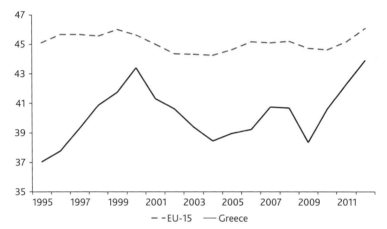

Figure 4.3   General government revenue (% GDP)

Source: AMECO Database.

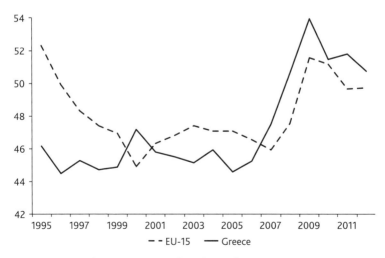

Figure 4.4   General government expenditure (% GDP)

Source: AMECO Database.

Compositional issues also arise on the expenditure side. Figure 4.5 is quite revealing, showing that Greece spends much more than the EU average on the military, and much less on health and education. Any account of Greece's high debt must include some reference not only to military expenditure but also the socialization of the debts of private sector firms, the costs associated with the organization of the Olympic Games,[87] the large infrastructural projects (notably in transport), and the support given to the banking sector after the crisis.[88] In modernizing accounts, bankers, constructors, military procurers and a host of other groups are rarely the targets of the sectionalist and populist critique. But they were most certainly central to the economic strategy of all modernizing governments in the pre-crisis years.

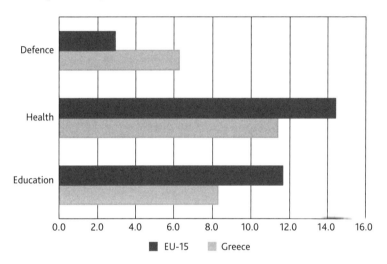

Figure 4.5   Structure of general government expenditure by function (2008)

Source: OECD, Government at a Glance 2011.

Notes: Bars show the percentage of total government expenditure corresponding to each government function. For EU 15, percentages are calculated as the average across all EU 15 countries.

The problem of tax evasion cannot be reduced to the organizational incompetence of the tax authorities. Stathakis' (2010) account of the formation of 'legal' tax evasion coalitions is both a more functional and a more convincing explanation. Sections of the middle class and even the working class were crucial to the formation of what Gramsci calls a historical bloc. Public sector employment can also be seen as a means of compensating for low social transfers – in other words, as a response to the issue of inequality inherent in all market economies, and an attempt to tie in the interests of capitalists to those of the middle classes and sections of the working class. For the small- and medium-sized enterprises that dominate the Greek economy, the availability of cheap credit and plentiful supplies of immigrant (mostly uninsured) labour also helped to enlarge the basis of support for the ruling bloc.

Such a historical bloc may be obscured by ideological narratives, but it can hardly remain a secret. Its roots go way back, as the extract at the beginning of this chapter, and that of Streeck below, make abundantly clear:

> As far as Greece is concerned, European politicians were well aware of the outstanding historical bills that had accrued since the end of the military dictatorship: a distribution of wealth reminiscent of Latin America; a practically tax-exempt upper class; and a democratic state that had no choice but to borrow the resources that its rich citizens had stashed abroad from the 'markets' or other states, so that the 'old money' could peacefully remain 'old money', and the new money could be used to buy the support of a growing middle class with its increasingly northern-orientated consumption norms.
>
> That no one took exception to this at the time may be due to the fact that the sole alternative, after the end of military rule in 1974, would have been a radical remodelling of Greek society, perhaps along the lines of Emilia–Romagna, then under Eurocommunist rule. However, no one in northern Europe nor the US was prepared to risk this, any more than in Portugal after the Carnation Revolution, in Spain after Franco, and least of all in 1970s Italy, where the Communist Party under Enrico Berlinguer abstained from participating in the government so as not to provoke a military coup like in Chile. Streeck (2012: 66)

All the above is hidden in the dominant narrative: both the winners and losers of established arrangements, and how alternative arrangements – with a different configuration of winners and losers – were effectively blocked. There is a place for populism even in our alternative narrative. But the line of causation is very different. It is not that a potentially dynamic, essentially neoliberal, economy was effectively blocked by the forces of populism. Rather, the weaknesses of the neoliberal economy had to be filled in with populist elements to shore up class alliances and the legitimacy of the system as a whole.[89]

Debt was a problem, but after the 1970s crisis (as we have seen) the whole neoliberal order was involved in 'borrowing from the future' in an attempt to alleviate distributional conflict and thus postpone an ultimate resolution to the political question that stemmed from this. Fiscal crises do not generally stem from exogenous episodes of fiscal irresponsibility. Rather, they reflect the existence of deeper underlying fractures. In this light, Greece's fiscal crisis cannot be seen as a qualitatively different phenomenon from the existence of private sector debt, and the 'excesses' of the financial sector, in other economies.

Both distributional and political conflict was bound to be accentuated after the crisis, not least because the question was now more forcibly posed: who was to pay for the fact that previous arrangements were no longer sustainable, and which social contracts (explicit or implicit) needed to be redrawn? We have argued that, since 1945, the Greek ruling elite have been remarkably successful in preserving their privileges, profits and power. This leaves open the possibility of a very different answer to the 'why Greece first?' question: it was a political decision to transform the crisis into an opportunity, and provide new foundations for the preservation of the status of ruling elites.

WHO PAYS?

In the prosperous 1960s, western economies bought social cohesion by making extravagant promises on pensions and healthcare. Slowing growth, exacerbated by the recent crisis and bank bailout, have raised public debt substantially. Government promises have become unaffordable in several industrial countries. Because governments need to borrow, they will try to renegotiate pensions and healthcare commitments, while continuing to service debt. Again, the appearance of favouring the rich investors at the expense of the wider public cannot but erode support for property rights.

To restore the system's legitimacy, industrial economies have to restore opportunity to the middle class, by improving education and creating the support structures that allow people to train for, obtain and keep good jobs. They also have to explain why some government promises are more equal than others and show that not only the plutocrats benefit. These are not easy tasks but they are essential to the survival of functioning market economies.[90]

We do not share Raghuram Rajan's views (above) about 'extravagant promises', or his focus on property rights. But his intelligent account, in a period in which enlightened elite accounts are at a premium, points to the fact that beyond the debt contract societies have many other contracts that need addressing. Recall that one of the theses, set out in the Introduction of this book, is the lack of plasticity in the post-crisis capitalist system – a factor that underlies the structural nature of the crisis in late capitalism. Governments of all stripes, especially in the Eurozone, were unable or unwilling to incorporate even the smallest of subsets of the demands stemming from the opposition to the policies of austerity. An agenda on education and jobs, let alone good ones, was nowhere in sight.

Perhaps the most curious aspect is the failure of social democrats to turn the crisis into an opportunity to return to a different economic and social agenda. In the Greek case, the PASOK government, elected in October 2009, could perhaps have led the way in this exercise of reappropriation. This would have entailed giving an answer regarding the existing social contracts that needed either to be preserved, merely renegotiated or abrogated. It would also have necessitated a democratic dialogue on the question of who pays – some kind of compromise between the demands of creditors and the needs of society – in order to provide a wider legitimacy for the difficult decisions to be made. At the very least this would have had to deal with tax evasion and broadening the tax base. PASOK's commitment to this cause, restated before and after the 2009 election, was barely credible given how often the promise had been made by all governments since 1974.[91]

Dealing with the tax question or, for that matter, how the Greek state organizes its procurements or selects public investment projects, would have required a willingness to break with the financial and economic elites that had dominated Greece since the war. But PASOK, along with most other parties of social democracy, had removed popular mobilization from its political armoury long ago. Before the election, PASOK promised that financing was available for a different, more Keynesian, strategy, but it seemed unaware that such a shift did not just provide a different technocratic solution to the crisis. It would have involved not just a rupture with domestic elites, but European ones as well.

In May 2010, during the run-up to the first adjustment programme, PASOK did not seem to be able to home in on a credible negotiating stance. It veered dangerously from claiming that no outside help was necessary to actually exaggerating the nature of the problem.[92] As the likelihood of a Greek bailout increased, Greek negotiators were unable (or perhaps unwilling) to point to the joint responsibility of lender and borrower in any debt crisis, or the fault lines within the Eurozone architecture (discussed in Chapter 3). The fact that German surpluses were the other side of the coin from Greek deficits, or that German banks had gained from financing the Greek current account deficit were not subjects to be brought up in polite conversation.

It is exceptionally difficult to respond to a serious debt crisis without control of your own money supply. Since monetary policy in a monetary union is carried out at the supranational level, one would have thought that this called for a joint response to any member state's debt crisis. Such reticence was to be repeated by other governments of the South in the following years. Mario Monti, with the larger clout provided by the weight of the Italian economy (not to mention the level of its debt), also conspicuously abstained from demanding that the North also needed to make adjustments if the crisis was to be managed. By the time Mariano Rajoy was asking Germany to take expansionary measures, in January 2013, Germany was already committed to its own austerity budget.[93]

The PASOK government failed to argue for a European collective solution to what was, as quickly became obvious, a European-wide debt problem. It seemed happy to go along with a case-by-case solution, and refused to seek allies in southern Europe for a different approach – one based on a more collective and solidaristic approach. Indeed, after the Greek bailout, and despite the onerous terms, the Greek political establishment would praise Europe's expression of solidarity with Greece. Worse still, before the bailout was agreed PASOK threatened to turn to the IMF should such help not be forthcoming from the Europeans. It was an idle threat, if it was actually meant to be taken seriously, as the turn to the IMF sealed the victory of the case-by-case approach that the majority of European elites in any case preferred.

In the light of all this it is difficult not to turn towards a more cynical interpretation, where the element of class instinct prevails. PASOK leaders seem to have reached an implicit bargain with European leaders. The interests of creditors, and northern European banks in particular, would be protected in the bailout – not least because the Troika would set the priorities of the adjustment programmes – while the political and economic privileges of Greek elites would be shored up as much as possible by the availability of finance while the adjustment programmes lasted (Dragasakis, 2012). The crisis would then be turned into an opportunity to finish the neoliberal modernizing project in terms of reducing wages and pensions, dismantling labour protection, and undertaking an even more radical programme of privatization.

As was the case with the analysis of the Eurozone crisis, we can include elements from the structural incompetence hypothesis. PASOK leaders, and in this they were not helped by their team of economists, seemed to have seriously underestimated the economic dynamics of the programme and the threat posed by the debt trap. The size of the recession, to which we shall shortly turn, seems to have caught them unawares. Years of trumpeting the virtues of the free market and the dynamism of entrepreneurship must have blunted the analytical capacities of PASOK's economic team. Cognitive locking was clearly a factor, and not only with respect to economic matters. The PASOK leadership also seemed to miscalculate the extent to which the structural adjustment programme and the debt trap would undermine most of the party's established pillars of social and political support. There seemed to be little awareness of how IMF programmes elsewhere had led to the collapse of existing political and social arrangements. They were perhaps unable to contemplate the scale of the political collapse that would ensue for PASOK.

From the perspective of the modernizing dominant narrative, the mistake in the run-up to the bailout was that not enough corrective measures were taken early enough. It is a moot point whether a lighter dose of the austerity approach carried out after May 2010 would have averted, rather than postponed, the bailout. In any case, PASOK modernizers would later claim that this course was unavailable because people were not psychologically prepared for the severity of the crisis, and the 'sacrifices' needed to overcome it. Greeks, it seems, had to pass through their 'Lehman Brothers moment', if they were to be reconciled to the new realities.

Within elite thinking, then, the main debate seems to have been about the timing of the austerity response. The objective social and political conditions needed to place a very different resolution onto the agenda were not in place in 2010. It would take the implementation of the austerity programmes, and their economic and social consequences with which we end this chapter, to change this around.

ECONOMIC AND SOCIAL CONSEQUENCES OF AUSTERITY

The austerity imposed on Greece was brutal at the macroeconomic level and unrelenting in its deepening of the neoliberal structural reform agenda. It is difficult to escape the conclusion that Greece presented itself as guinea pig and a warning to other economies to take 'appropriate' measures on their own in good time. The economic results were abysmal, leading to year after year of recession, rising unemployment and a vicious cycle of austerity–recession–more austerity.

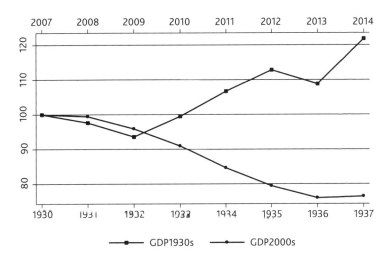

Figure 4.6   Index of real GDP per capita: 1930s and 2000s compared

Source: AMECO database (November 2012); Kostelenos, G., et al. (2007).

Figure 4.6 shows that Greece's recession bears little resemblance in severity to that which it experienced in the 1930s. It was, on the contrary, far more similar to the experience of the US during the Great Depression. The fall in income in Greece, compared to the US of the earlier period, was less steep in the initial period, but more persistent and with a more delayed (projected) recovery (see Figure 4.7). Industrial production (manufacturing, mining, electricity) fell by 23.3 per cent between October 2008 and October 2012, widening the gap between Greece and its EU partners (see Figure 4.8). There

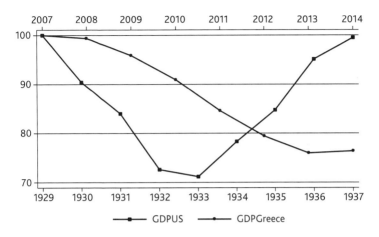

Figure 4.7   US 1930s compared to Greece 2000s – index real per capita GDP

Source: AMECO database (November 2012); US Census Bureau, *Statistical Abstract of the United States, Selected Per Capita Income and Product Items in Current and Real* (1996) Dollars.

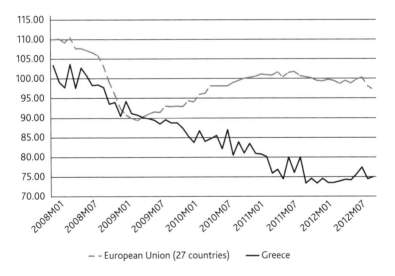

Figure 4.8   Index of industrial production

Source: EUROSTAT, Short-term Business Statistics.

are no official data in Greece on the number of new enterprises or those that have closed down. Of course, in the years after 2010 a walk down any street would have been evidence enough of the scale of closures in the retail sector. Wage and pension cuts led to a sharp fall in consumption. This is reflected in the Retail Trade Turnover Index, where the cumulative loss between 2008 and 2012 was over 40 per cent (Figure 4.9).

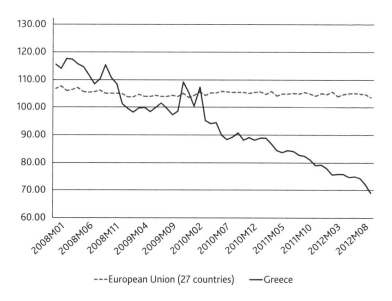

--- European Union (27 countries)   —— Greece

Figure 4.9   Retail trade index of deflated turnover, 2008–present (2005 = 100)

Source: EUROSTAT, Short-term Business Statistics.

The professional organizations of small enterprises in Greece have estimated that between 2010 and 2012 almost 60,000 enterprises closed down each year. According to the estimates of a European Commission study, the number of enterprises in Greece shrunk by 100,000 between 2008 and 2012 (see Figure 4.10). Matters were not helped by the crisis of the Greek banking sector, which was exposed, not as elsewhere to toxic derivatives, but to public sector bonds.[94] While the process of recapitalization of the banking sector dragged on, especially through 2012 as the Troika delayed payments to ensure compliance with its increasingly unrealistic programme, liquidity collapsed and firms faced a credit crisis of epic proportions (see Figure 4.11).

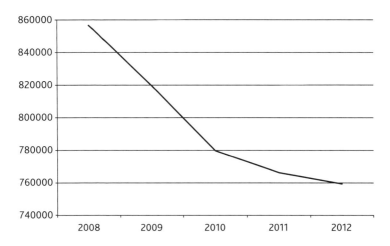

Figure 4.10   Number of enterprises, Greece

Source: Database for the Annual Report on European SMEs, SME Performance Review 2012, European Commission.

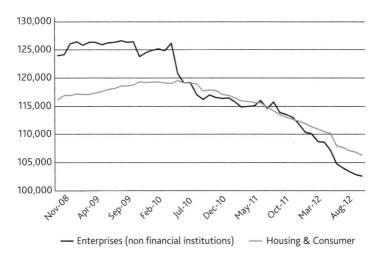

— Enterprises (non financial institutions)   — Housing & Consumer

Figure 4.11   Credit to domestic private sector by domestic MFIs (outstanding amount, € million)

Source: Bank of Greece.

At one level, the above results were quite predictable. Thirty years of neoliberal economics seems to have dimmed peoples' memories about how large recessions play out. For some time central Keynesian concepts, such as the multiplier, were barely taught in economics departments, and had almost vanished from public debate. The issue resolves around the final reduction in income of a given reduction in government expenditure or increase in taxes. Any number greater than 1 for the multiplier implies that the reduction in income is greater than the size of the initial contraction, thereby leading to a downward spiral and the so-called debt trap. However, by the autumn of 2012 the IMF was accepting, in its annual *World Economic Outlook*, that the multipliers assumed in many austerity programmes were in fact too small; that instead of 0.5, the correct order of magnitude may lie somewhere between 0.9 and 1.7. Needless to say, this was not a small correction in the impact of a given reduction in state expenditure on national income. In the Eurozone economies in particular, higher multipliers should have been factored in because there was no available looser monetary policy to offset fiscal consolidation, and nearly all economies were undertaking such consolidation at the same time (Holland and Portes, 2012). To these general considerations we may add that Greece is in fact a small closed, and not open, economy, a factor that also works to increase the size of the multiplier.

Whatever the size of the multiplier, the real problem was that nearly all the orthodox channels of recovery from austerity were blocked off (Boyer, 2012). It was difficult to believe that any austerity programme was to be the last, as people were very aware that the Eurozone was failing to come up with a comprehensive response to the crisis (Chapter 3). Moreover, it did not take long before the existence of a debt trap was obvious to all but the most sanguine of observers. And so it proved, as one programme followed another despite various haircuts and attempts to reduce the burden of interest payments (see timeline in Appendix).

In this context, there was little reason to go out and spend, let alone invest. Nor did interest rates in the real economy fall by nearly enough in the South of the Eurozone. One of the outcomes of the crisis was the severing of even the common monetary policy of the Eurozone, as the cheap money policy of the ECB was not easily transmitted into the periphery. The fear that Greece (and other countries for that matter) may need further assistance, and may actually leave or be expelled from the euro was never squashed once and for all, with obvious consequences for interest rates.

Furthermore, any positive effects on competitiveness from falling real wages and more flexible labour practices were always likely to be smothered in such a deep recession by the Keynesian effects of falling demand and closing factories and shops.

The other obvious consequence was rising unemployment. After the signing of the first adjustment programme, employment fell, according to the Labour Force Survey of the Hellenic Statistical Authority, by about 688,000 (up to the third quarter of 2012). During the same period, unemployment skyrocketed from 11.8 per cent to 24.8 per cent. Youth unemployment in particular has always been high in Greece, but by the autumn of 2012 it stood at 56.6 per cent. More than 1.2 million people were unemployed during the third quarter of 2012; 62.6 per cent of them were long-term unemployed.

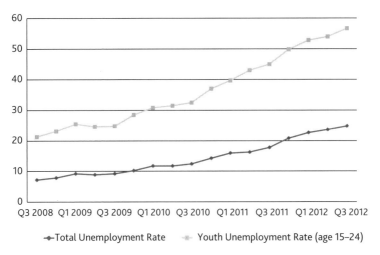

Figure 4.12   Unemployment in Greece, 2008–12 (% of labour force)

Source: Labour Force Survey, Hellenic Statistical Authority (EL.STAT).

The rise in unemployment was a critical cog in driving the recession ever deeper. For those still in work, a new wave of labour market reforms ensured both lower wages and worsening conditions of employment. As a result, according to the official data published by the Labour Inspectorate, flexible labour relations became the rule. While in 2009 full-time jobs constituted almost 80 per cent of new hiring, by 2012 they were only 56 per cent. Even worse, there was a sharp increase in changes to employment contracts. During the first half of 2010 there were only 60 cases of a unilateral change to job rotation; by the first half of 2012 there were 7,350 such cases (see Figure 4.13).

The social consequences of austerity were greater still. The rise in poverty levels (see Figure 4.14) reflected not only the increased

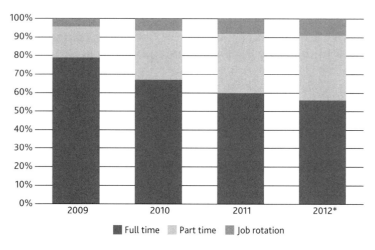

Figure 4.13   Employment status in new hirings (% of total)

Source: Labour Inspectorate, Press Release 18 July 2012.

Note: * 1st half.

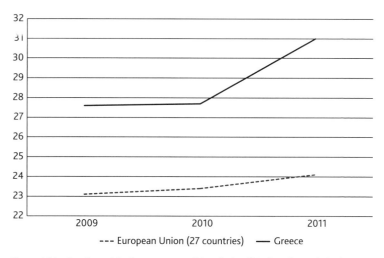

Figure 4.14   People at risk of poverty or social exclusion (% of total population)

Source: EUROSTAT, Income and Living Conditions.

number of unemployed but the working poor too, as reductions in the minimum wage brought down most other wages as well. Pensioners were also severely at risk, as a result of successive cuts even for those earning pensions barely above the poverty line. All these groups were unable to meet the frequent tax hikes, and increasingly they did not even have access to heating as taxes on fuel grew inordinately. Even though there are no official data about homelessness, it was a new phenomenon that became more than apparent in the larger cities. One study[95] estimated that between 2009 and 2011 the number of homeless people increased by 25 per cent. For the first time since the war, Greece faced a humanitarian crisis.

CONCLUSION

Apart from the economic and humanitarian consequences, there were important implications for Greece's social formation. The first austerity government of George Papandreou had tried to suggest that the necessary adjustment, given that the problem was basically fiscal in nature, mainly concerned the state and public sector workers. Such deception was an important political gambit in trying to divide public sector workers from those in the private sector. But even before the signing of the first adjustment programme, Dominique Strauss Kahn, the then head of the IMF, was making it clear to anybody who would listen that the austerity programme was an exercise in internal devaluation. Given that devaluation of the currency was unavailable, it would require a severe dose of austerity to get Greek wages down to competitive levels. By the time of the second austerity programme, the IMF was making it clear that Greece should consider its competitors to include countries such as Bulgaria, and that consequently wage levels in the private sector still had some way to fall. The ideological underpinning now shifted: those in the private sector should not complain about falling wages when there were so many unemployed without any wage at all.

The ranks of the unemployed were also, of course, frequently replenished from the self-employed and those losing their small businesses. So the process of internal devaluation was in fact leading to a proletarization of the Greek social formation. While in Chapter 2 we argued that since 1974 the number of the self-employed was slowly, but steadily, converging on European norms, the adjustment programmes were forcing a far faster and far more brutal convergence. The number of people who had literarily nothing to support them other than their labour power increased enormously in the three years after 2010. Again, there is logic to the madness. And it is a logic that is more consistent with the class instinct hypothesis than that of the structural incompetence one.

Falling wages and pensions, savage cuts to social expenditure, Great Depression levels of unemployment and a brutal process of proletarization would have led to resistance even if there had been some sign that the programme, on its own terms at least, was working. But there was precious little evidence of an end to the downward spiral that the austerity programmes had initiated. As we saw at the end of the previous chapter: the class instinct hypothesis may be the one that assumes the greater amount of rationality on behalf of the elites, but that does not mean that rational strategies may not lead to irrational and unforeseen outcomes – not least because of an underestimation of the strength of the opposition, to which we now turn.

5
The Underdogs Strike Back

If economic crises are difficult to predict, the same could be said for the various forms of social resistance and political radicalization that follow. In the initial post-crisis period there is always the hope that what seems to be a crisis is no more than a temporary blip. Even when the structural features of the crisis become a little more apparent, there is always a chance that appropriate policies will lead to a speedy return to the *status quo ante*.[96] More important still is the fact that, as any crisis deepens, the element of fear comes increasingly into play: that however bad things are, they can always get worse; that social mobilization and political radicalization can lead to conflict and disorder, the cost of which may well be borne by those that have already fared worse in the crisis; that the powerful have all the best cards and that resistance is pointless.

In the current crisis deeper considerations also came in to play. The neoliberal project did not only result in vast gains for capital and those at the top of the income and wealth distributions. A critical element in the whole exercise, as we have argued, was undermining at the institutional level the ability of those at the bottom end to resist by organizing collectively. At the same time, social developments, and those at the level of production, had created new forms of fragmentation that further weakened collective responses. At the ideological level, neoliberal hegemony entailed a marginalization of politics as a form of self-realization, as well as a means to economic and social advancement. In short, the struggle between capital and labour is not only over the spoils of war, but the very terrain of the battle. Neoliberal initiatives of the previous period had been geared to restricting the ability of 'the other side' to respond in any future conflict.

All these factors may have played some role in the initially anaemic response 'from below' after 2008. This encouraged elites to trust what we have called their class instinct. Rather than seeking out compromise, or even a rebalancing of the neoliberal order, they pursued a further deepening of that order. One can debate the extent to which more rigorous and timely reactions would have been able to change the agenda to any great extent. But they would surely have led to a more cautious response on behalf of the elites. For all that, social and political responses from below were not long in coming. Moreover, once they came there was evidence of an inner dynamic which tended to transcend the issue of how best to react to the symptoms of the crisis. To be sure, the question of 'who should pay for the crisis' was at the heart of most protests. But, at the same time, social movements and political forces were able to open up not only a democratic agenda, but also one of alternative consumption and production prototypes that potentially provided a challenge to the neoliberal order at a far deeper level.

The quality and scope of democracy, the role of financial markets, and consumption and production prototypes are the types of issues that 'modernization' theory was supposed to have more or less permanently settled. In the case of Greece, Diamandouros' analysis (already discussed in Chapter 1) suggested that only an 'underdog culture' expressed a deep lack of faith 'towards capitalism and the workings of the market' (1994: 80). Moreover, this culture's ambiguous relationship 'to the liberal, western model of socio-economic change', materializes 'itself historically with *the tendency to search for and experiment with "alternative" roads for development*' (ibid: 54, our emphasis). Leaving aside the small issue that the latter would seem to deposit nearly the whole of the Left (in more or less all of its manifestations since the Industrial Revolution) within an underdog culture, it was always unlikely that faith in the workings of the market and eschewing experimentation with alternatives would offer much solace to the victims of the crisis.

And so it proved. After 2010 the scale and nature of protest in Greece, as elsewhere in the Eurozone, is enough to expose the ideological content of modernization perspectives. The underdogs struck back. Populist, and even reactionary, responses were never absent as the phenomenon of the neo-fascist Golden Dawn Party in Greece amply testifies. But more often than not, those involved in social and political protest were aware that there was no easy return to the *status quo ante*. Far from being merely populist or outdated protests harking back to some traditional Valhalla, there developed out of the various forms of resistance a challenge to some of the central priorities and methods of the neoliberal order.

Our account here – of how the 'underdogs' struck back in Greece – will hopefully do justice to the diversity, in both means and ends, of the response, while also pointing to the cross-fertilization of both themes and aspirations from similar responses elsewhere.

THE RETURN OF STREET POLITICS?

We begin with three manifestations of protest that were not direct responses to the policies of austerity and the adjustment programmes agreed with the Troika. At one level all three could be marginalized, given the perspective of this book, as monothematic in nature; responding to, respectively, police brutality, ecological degradation and the rights of immigrants. But this would be a mistake, for they brought to the fore many of the issues that would later feature in anti-austerity protests such as human rights, democracy and conditions in the workplace.

More importantly, all three to some extent represented a breach with much of the politics of the post-1974 period in Greece. They involved non-conventional actors willing to use non-conventional means. To a large extent, but not entirely, political parties and unions were sidelined, and this entailed a set of commitments that were less state-centred, or indeed anti-state. The repertoire of means was also enlarged in a more confrontational, often violent, direction. Not surprisingly, public opinion and political parties were strongly divided on how to respond. Within the dominant narrative, the response was largely predictable – the main issue was violence, the main concern was avoiding giving in to sectionalist interests. More interestingly, these protests divided the Left, not just between parties but also within, and, as we shall see, the response to these manifestations of protest was of critical importance to the issue of political hegemony once anti-austerity politics reached centre-stage.

The December Events[97]

On the night of 6 December 2008, a young schoolboy, Alexandros Grigoropoulos, was murdered in cold blood by a policeman in the centre of Athens. In the following two days there were demonstrations and riots in Athens, with unprecedented levels of violence. But soon the protests spread throughout Greece, even reaching small towns with 2–3 thousand inhabitants. The targets of much of the violence were not only police stations, but also banks and private property in general. Stones and pieces of pavement were the usual weapons of these attacks, but the use of Molotov cocktails was not rare. The actors were predominantly schoolchildren and students, but there was considerable support, active or passive, from older generations as well.

The scale of the protests took everybody by surprise; especially since at the time Greeks were being assured that their economy was relatively more protected from the world crisis that had erupted only three months earlier. From the beginning there was a conflict of naming. Given the scale and intensity of the protest, many spoke in terms of an uprising or an eruption; others were likely to stick with riots.[98] Such naming conflicts reflect different evaluative stances. However, as Seferiades and Johnston (2012: 3) argue, one cannot go very far with a polarity that either idealizes such violent collective action or sees it as a 'pathological' dysfunction. As the same authors also point out, such action involves 'both rational negotiation and strategic creativity'.

One of the targets of discontent was Greece's hierarchical and divisive education system. On the one hand larger numbers had been leaving high school at an earlier stage, and on the other those that remained faced a tough regime of rote learning and crammers in the rat race to enter university. The promise to raise expenditure on public education had been consistently betrayed by both major parties, which had, instead, focused their energies on 'reforms' to tie education closer to the needs of production and allow the private sector a greater role in tertiary education. The voice of the Greek youth was heard throughout the world, even leading to Italian and French conservatives withdrawing, temporarily at least, proposals for 'educational reform' that they feared could lead to similar protests.

Thus, the criticism that was often repeated, namely the lack of clear objectives, was only partially accurate. The movement expressed a generalized disaffection with Greece's past and, in retrospect, seems to have brought forward many of the issues that would feature after 2010. Most conservative accounts would later focus on the violence, but at the time most commentators understood that the unprecedented protests represented a cry of despair from Greece's young people.[99] In the previous decade the radical Left had been organizing around the issue of the '€700 generation'; a generation of young people facing not only low wages but insecure employment and poor pension prospects. The amount and quality of available jobs was an issue in Greece well before the arrival of the Troika and the rise of youth unemployment to unprecedented levels. It is no coincidence that at roughly the same time as the December events, Constantina Kouneva, an immigrant trade union leader from Bulgaria, was subject to a vitriolic attack leading to her being permanently scarred. The suspicion was that her attackers were acting on behalf of employers in an industry concentrating on subcontracting cleaning work to companies that allowed the worst possible labour conditions.

This was a generation that felt that its prospects were worse than those of their parents, thereby removing the psychological blanket that the ideal of progress has provided for capitalist societies in the past. From this perspective, and given the spontaneous nature of the events that unfolded,[100] the term uprising does not seem out of place.

Keratea

Keratea, a small town southeast of Athens, was for 128 days in the winter of 2010/2011 the centre of another movement of confrontational civil disobedience. The area had been scarred for many years with an open-cast refuse landfill to serve the more than 3 million inhabitants of the greater Athens region. When proposals were announced for a new sanitary disposal unit next to the old landfill, the opposition from local residents was determined and universal. People responded to their gut feeling that they had no control over either the value of their land or the natural wealth of their community. The local authority, schoolteachers and schoolchildren, community organizations and even the priesthood joined in the protests. Barricades were set up, trenches were dug, the machinery of the construction firms was sabotaged and there were violent clashes with the police on a daily basis. Priests were even caught on camera blessing young people and their Molotov cocktails!

It would be fair to say that the protestors lacked a clear conception of the wider problem of Athens' refuse disposal. But at the centre of the dispute was not only the issue of ecological degradation, but of trust. The not unfounded fear of the local population was that proposals that initially included more state-of-the-art technology would be subject to downgrading as the real costs of such initiatives became apparent. More importantly, people doubted that the state would give much weight to their concerns after the project was completed, especially since the maintenance of large projects has been a perennial problem of the Greek state – the dilapidated state of many of the projects associated with Greece's organization of the Olympic Games in 2004 was evidence enough of this chronic inability.

The eventual compromise left the more ecologically sensitive disappointed, especially since it included a more corporate solution without a wider vision of how the problem of refuse could be addressed for the wider Athens area. But the worst consequences had been avoided for the community. People had been radicalized by the experience and Keratea came to symbolize the ability of communities to remain communities, and to react to an increasingly repressive neoliberal state through collective action.

Hypatia

At the beginning of 2011, 300 hundred or so immigrants started a hunger strike in Thessaloniki and Athens. Most were from those North African countries then facing open revolt in the 'Arab Spring'. A large number ended up in a building, previously a museum, named Hypatia. Their fight against deportation brought to the fore not only the issue of the rights of undocumented workers 'sans papiers', but the state of employment relations in general. It reminded people of the fact that the model of development in the years before the crisis had relied on such immigrant workers, whether or not they had the necessary legal documents. The fact that the state, with its own initiatives, was willing to underline their dispensability in the time of crisis, contributed to the worsening anti-immigrant climate, which had been rising in response to growing unemployment and the large flows of refugees fleeing to Greece in the hope of moving on to the rest of the EU. It was a climate that Golden Dawn was able to exploit for its own purposes, as the social consequences of the crisis continued to multiply.

For the state, those supporting the hunger strikes were political extremists who were more than willing to flirt with violence in order to flout the rule of law. In fact, an impressive movement of solidarity quickly developed that encompassed social groups and political organizations. The official trade union organizations, and even grassroot union initiatives known for their more radical agenda, were unwilling to offer much support until just before the end. A special role was played by hospital doctors who not only offered direct medical support, but sought to counter government propaganda – not least that stemming from the minister of health who claimed that the hunger strikers presented a 'medical time bomb' at the centre of the city.

Astonishingly, for all the government's attempt to blacken the name of the hunger strikers and their supporters, the movement was largely successful. The moral and humanitarian pressure resulted in no less than four ministers being involved in the final negotiations that reached a compromise. The hunger strikers were given temporary work permits, and the right to leave and re-enter the country.[101] What is more, the government agreed to decrease the number of national insurance stamps needed to have access to medical care for both immigrant *and* indigenous workers. The latter was an important card in highlighting the importance of overcoming the divisions within labour and helped counter the claims of the radical right that leftist protests ignored the needs of Greek workers. In the daily struggle, in which hunger strikers were constantly being taken back and forth between hospitals and Hypatia, often in a comatose state, the issue of dignity came into sharp focus. It was a theme that was to reoccur often as the austerity protests deepened in the following months. There is little doubt that those in the later protests owe a large debt to the hunger strikers who had demonstrated that even 'children of a lesser God' can organize themselves for successful political initiatives, and, even in the most difficult of circumstances, win.

*   *   *

The three protest movements above divided not only Greek society in general, but the parties of the Greek Left. It is difficult to believe that the rise of SYRIZA would have been anything like as impressive if it had not openly and vigorously supported all three. To be sure, other non-parliamentary parties and radical organizations (including those of the anarchists and anarchist affinity groups) were heavily involved as well. But SYRIZA was supposed to be a more conventional party, on the right of the orthodox communist party, the KKE. Moreover, its support led to widespread disagreement within SYRIZA, and especially within the largest party of the coalition, Synaspismos.

Thus, SYRIZA's stance seemed to be risky at the time; for many commentators, even foolhardy. It was not an easy choice given the conservative nature of Greek society. But SYRIZA managed to maintain a fine balance. It refused to accept that one should focus on the violence of the confrontations without examining the nature of the discontent that underlay it. It accepted that social movements always have spontaneous elements and a degree of autonomy from political parties. It argued that the role of the radical Left was not to oppose social polarization as such, but to provide a more political, and of course non-violent, vehicle for channelling protest towards strategies for social transformation.

The KKE's stance was radically different but hardly radical. Continuing a long tradition of not supporting social movements it does not control,[102] the KKE was hostile to the December events. It sought to ridicule all talk of an 'uprising', and attacked SYRIZA as opportunistically seeking to make overtures to anarchist elements. It was a mistake that it was to repeat later with the phenomenon of the town squares, with even more fateful political consequences. It seems to have forgotten one of the first rules of politics: those not taking sides in episodes of polarization risk political marginalization. The KKE was also seemingly unaware that social protests were bringing to the fore new actors, new means of political mobilization and new goals. There would be no necessity for any Left party to incorporate all these innovations in an uncritical fashion. But to ignore them was a sign of political sclerosis.

For years the KKE had been the dominant party on the Left – SYRIZA, and before that Synaspismos, was often the poor relation. In any fuller account of the eventual reversal of this relationship, the KKE's stance with respect to the protests discussed above will have to figure prominently.

ORGANIZING AGAINST AUSTERITY

Unions and General Strikes

The opposition to austerity and the Troika programmes began in earnest with the unions. The General Confederation of Greek Workers (GSEE) called for a general strike on 5 May 2010. On that day Athens, but Thessaloniki as well, saw massive demonstrations. However, in Athens a Molotov cocktail attack on the Marfin Bank in central Athens led to the tragic death of three banking workers who were trapped in the office. This was undoubtedly an important setback that broke, for a while at least, the momentum of the opposition. But the general strikes kept coming, numbering almost 30 up to the end of 2012. If we include about 500 other individual strike actions in 2011, and more than 700 in 2012, this adds up to an impressive response from the side of labour. Moreover, the focus was on job losses, unpaid wages, the imposition of job rotation and other forms of precarious employment schemes, with wages taking a back seat.

At one level the scale of the mobilizations is quite surprising. The GSEE had long been under the control of PASOK factions within trade union organizations (PASKE), although the power of the New Democracy factions (DAKE) was far from negligible. Both had close relationships with their party leadership, and on the whole failed to even keep up appearances with respect to the autonomous role of the labour movement. But both also had to walk a fine line between showing some results for their members while still providing the degree of control demanded by the leadership of their respective political party. Such a balancing act continued in the era of austerity. The GSEE ultimately bowed to pressures to be seen to be doing something, but singularly failed to provide the type of organization necessary for general strikes, and the level of coordination needed for other forms of action,[103] which would have convinced people that ending the policies of the government and the Troika was a serious goal.

In any case, the tone of the demonstrations was given by the Left, especially SYRIZA and the smaller leftist non-parliamentary parties.[104] Throughout 2011, general strikes were being called every five or six weeks, climaxing in the events of 19 and 20 October. On Wednesday the 19 October more than 1 million people filled the streets of Athens, Thessaloniki and other large towns in a show of strength unprecedented since 1974. The demonstrators were sailing in the slipstream of the town square mobilizations of the previous summer (covered in detail below), and the focus was far more political than before. The target was now clearly the PASOK government that had been reshuffled only a few months earlier. The demonstration had been far better organized and linked not only to strikes in the private sector but also a series of occupations of town halls, ministries and other public buildings. During the annual national parade of 28 October, demonstrators actively broke up the celebrations, renting their wrath on public officials, including the president of the Republic who had to make a speedy exit from the officials' podium. A few days later the PASOK government fell, to be replaced by that of Lucas Papademos (supported by PASOK, New Democracy and the far right LAOS). Papademos' government faced similar resistance and could only last until the summer of 2012, when two general elections were held in May and June.

In many respects, the Greek trajectory was to be repeated in the Iberian Peninsula some months later. The adoption of austerity, as part of an adjustment programme in the case of Portugal and in order to avoid such an eventuality in the case of Spain, did not lead to any linear rise in the Left. This was less surprising in Spain, but was more so in Portugal where both the communist party and the Left Bloc had been making headway in the years before the crisis. But something was moving at the social level, and as in Greece the town squares movement was not replacing labour militancy, but leading to an overall radicalization. On 15 September there were massive demonstrations against austerity and the Coelho government of an intensity not seen since May 1974, which led to the government taking back some of its proposed tax measures. A new peak was reached with the general strike of 14 November, coordinated with European-wide actions on the same day, which saw demonstrations in 39 towns against the visit of Angela Merkel. Furthermore, the action encompassed not just the usual suspects in the public sector and transport, but also in the private sector where participation ranged from 60 per cent to 100 per cent.[105] In the second half of 2012, Spain also witnessed a heightened level of labour resistance to the policies of austerity, with 14 November again being a critical date. As in Greece, the Spanish labour movement built on the experience of the town squares, and in particular the dynamism of the '15th of May Movement'. In effect 14 May was an Iberian general strike.

Such coordination was still far below what was needed to challenge the policies of the Eurozone. Thus, for instance, the 14 May mobilization was *not* a success in Greece. But it was suggestive of the possibilities that existed for the wider labour movement.

Can't Pay, Won't Pay[106]

Very soon after the first adjustment programme, a number of movements developed against a series of price hikes, notably with respect to tax increases, public transport and motorway tolls. These movements mobilized a large number of people from different backgrounds, many of them new to any form of political protest, and were able to exert considerable pressure on the governments of austerity.

Since the 1990s Greece's public infrastructural projects had been dominated by motorway construction. The contracts between the state and private construction companies had always been a bone of contention, given the favourable terms of most contracts for the private sector, which nevertheless consistently managed to overrun budgeted costs. Often the contract allowed construction companies to set up tolls as a means to finance not only maintenance but new motorways before their completion. As a result, numerous toll stations were set up all over Greece, mainly close to suburban areas near Athens and other big cities. This provoked outrage in some communities, which formed the first local 'committees against tolls' in the late 2000s.

Shortly after the signing of the first Memorandum of Understanding with the Troika, the construction companies raised toll prices. This decision proved to be a catalyst for the creation of a significant movement throughout Greece. Local committees came together and formed the 'Pan-Hellenic Steering Committee against Tolls'. These committees organized a successful nationwide information campaign and undertook a series of militant actions, occupying toll booths. For a couple of months, in late 2010, almost no driver paid tolls – everybody got out of their vehicles and raised the bars.

The government tried to cool down the protests by cancelling the toll price rises, but changing the terms of the contracts was out of the question. In early 2011 a law was passed, according to which non-payment was turned into a criminal offense leading to hefty fines. At the same time police were dispatched to every toll station to monitor drivers' compliance. After that, the movement against tolls receded. But it had managed to cancel price rises, a fact not lost on those fighting against similar price rises in the public transport of major cities. More importantly perhaps, the movement had made large numbers aware of the nature of the contracts the state had reached with private constructors.

In Autumn 2011, the Greek Government decided to impose a new tax, due to another shortfall in state revenues. This was a special property tax, levied through electricity bills. It was quickly named 'haratsi', thus associating it with the loathed poll tax imposed in the time of the Ottoman Empire. Strictly speaking, however, the tax was not a poll tax: it is related to the size and age of the building and the area where it is located. But the decision to collect it through electricity bills was particularly pernicious, and as would be eventually proven under the pressure of the protest movement, unconstitutional. It was a decision that, in effect, acknowledged the inability of the tax officials to raise property taxes. But cutting off poor peoples' supplies of electricity in a time of crisis was a source of widespread social discontent. Quite rapidly, people started organizing against the haratsi, which many could not pay in the aftermath of wage, or pension, cuts and other increases in taxes. The 'commissions against the poll tax' also encompassed a diverse range of people: not just committed activists, but lawyers who provided advice to people fearing the worse as a result of nonpayment and the expertise to mount legal challenges, and workers from the Public Power Corporation who refused to cut the power to poorer people, and more generally in the poorer areas.

Finally, special mention should be given to a series of mobilizations in the area of health. One of the most series casualties of the austerity policies was the growing number of people losing their access to medicine and pharmaceutical services as they effectively became deinsured. Access to such services, irrespective of income, or employment or residency status, became the focus of health unions operating in the public sector. In particular the Federation of Hospital Doctors took a number of important initiatives on these lines, climaxing with the establishment of Wednesdays as a day of free access to health care in hospitals for the uninsured. Hospital workers also opposed the imposition of a €5 flat-rate charge on all outpatients with their campaign 'Won't Pay €5 for the NHS'.

THE PHENOMENON OF THE TOWN SQUARES

None of the above movements and protests 'managed, independent of their outcome, to find such as a response, to engage so many people and to threaten to such a degree the strategic management of the crisis and with such implications at the European level' (Papadatos-Anagnostopoulos, forthcoming) as did the movement associated with Syntagma Square in the heart of Athens.[107] For two months in the summer of 2011, Greece's version of Los Indignados of the Puerta del Sol in Madrid,[108] came to be the focus of the struggle against austerity. In the context of the evolving Eurozone crisis, it was also a source of anxiety for elites, and of hope for protest movements, throughout the world.

The Aganaktismenoi, as the indignant were known in Greece, managed to break with the monothematic nature of many of the protest movements that had gone before. As the movement gained strength, there was a growing self-recognition not only of links to events in North Africa but also of the European significance of what was going on. It helped that the early far-right presence in the town squares was quickly restricted, if never completely marginalized.[109] This went hand-in-hand with an expanded agenda. The call was not merely to bring an end to austerity, but for the return to democracy, underlying the importance of what we have discussed as the political moment of the crisis.[110] In this light, the slogan 'to change everything' represents less a populist afterglow, as the dominant narrative was quick to claim, and more a recognition that the crisis went far deeper than its economic aspects. The social composition of the participants was also far wider than in many of the earlier conflicts, with (as discussed in Chapter 4) significant support from sections of the *déclassé* middle class that felt betrayed by successive governments of the two established political parties. Despite extraordinary levels of state repression, including unprovoked daily doses of tear gas attacks, this broad movement managed to mobilize millions in Athens and in the other cities where the movement quickly spread, while the level of its support amongst the population reached unprecedented levels.[111]

None of this could have been predicted in 25 May 2011 when the first heterogeneous gatherings, of all ages and classes, with many unemployed among them, began to converge not only on Syntagma Square, but also on that of the White Tower in Thessaloniki and many others throughout the country.[112] They had responded to a call organized seemingly spontaneously through the social media network; on a model previously tried out in 2007 with the 'silent' movement against the inability of the state to deal with summer fires that ravage the countryside almost on a perennial basis. Nor could it have been predicted that so many people, from public intellectuals to the unemployed, would be engaged on a daily basis in protests, discussions about the nature of democracy, or decision-making assemblies about the priorities of the movement. It proved to be a movement that in many ways surpassed what had gone before, being confrontational without being violent, encompassing more participatory forms of politics, and thereby changing peoples' conceptions about the nature of politics and its ability to influence social reality (Douzinas, 2011).

The daily experience of the squares was interspersed with occasional peaks of generalized and widespread mobilization that were, by their very size and stridency, able to significantly influence political developments. The first of these on 15 June encompassed a labour mobilization of such proportions that the square turned into a sea of people stretching down all the roads leading into Syntagma Square. The police attempted to break up the protest with waves of tear gas attacks, but failed to dent the resolve of the demonstrators: after each retreat from the square, its 'rightful' occupants returned.

What was remarkable was that, in the main, the participants were drawn from way beyond the pool of left-wing activists that had some experience of these tactics. Perhaps for this very reason, in recognition that 15 June presented a new phase in the opposition to austerity, the Papandreou government tottered. Papandreou's overtures to the New Democracy opposition were rebuffed, but nobody was in doubt that the days of his government were numbered. The events of 28 and 29 June in response to the vote in parliament on the new medium-term financial strategy were met, if anything, with an even greater degree of violence by the police. On that day, the gap between an actually existing 'nation' and the national government widened as never before. The fall of the

Papandreou government, after the demonstrations of 28 October during the annual parade to celebrate Greece's refusal to bow to the demands of Italy in 1940, can be seen as an aftershock of what took place in late June. For all the media attempts to portray the protests in unpatriotic terms, it was astonishing how many were now convinced that it was the demonstrators who represented some form of continuity with Greece's best moments of national independence and anti-fascism, and not the politicians officiating in the parades.

The town squares had contributed to the fall of one government of austerity and the instability of the next. But they had not managed to stop the course of austerity policies in Greece. Perhaps for this reason most of the momentum had petered out by the summer of 2012. It was, of course, a momentum that was to be taken up by the political Left, to which we shall shortly turn. But before that we should point to the lasting effect of the movement, not least for the practices of the Left itself.

The town squares movement had started off as one that was, in many ways, anti-political. In particular, it was openly hostile to most forms of political intermediation of existing parties. But the Left, not only SYRIZA but the smaller parties of the extra-parliamentary Left, had gradually participated as equals while largely accepting the autonomy of the movement. It had also started off as anti-union, but had eventually joined forces with labour, especially during the events of 15, 28 and the 29 June; a meeting that, as we have seen, enabled it to influence the course of political developments.

It was a movement that was in turn ignored and ridiculed by the private media, able to bypass that media with its own networks, and to stake out its own ground in opposition not only to the official media but the dominant parties of the establishment. Above all, it helped a section of the Left to look at politics afresh, to re-evaluate public goods, to seek new forms of political participation, and, above all, to seek to recover lost ground at the level of progressive values. And all this from a movement that in its initial stages seemed to have adopted a superficial and moralizing understanding of the crisis and the policies of the governments of austerity.

All this was lost on the leadership of the KKE, which, as in earlier instances of protests against austerity, chose to dissociate itself from the movement. It proved to be a fateful error. For all their dynamism, the squares had not been able to block the austerity bulldozer. But the ground had been opened up to any political force that could offer some hope that the policies of austerity could be finally reversed in order to set the course for a new economic, social and democratic agenda.

THE SYRIZA PHENOMENON

The rise of the Coalition of the Radical Left, or SYRIZA, has not gone unnoticed. For a time, between the two elections of 2012 on 6 May and 17 June, it actually seemed possible that a party that in the previous election in 2009 had received 4.5 per cent of the vote might actually win. The response from elites throughout the world, from Angela Merkel to Christine Lagarde of the IMF, was telling. A victory for SYRIZA would spell the end of Greece's participation in the euro, massive capital flight, bank runs, mass poverty and possibly the opening of the heavens and a deluge of frogs as well. Domestic elites were closely attuned to the same themes, and promoted a campaign of fear not seen since the civil war.

In the end SYRIZA was narrowly defeated, gaining 26.9 per cent of the vote to New Democracy's 29.6 per cent. The once mighty PASOK came in a poor third, with 12.2 per cent. Antonis Samaras formed a coalition government, with the support of PASOK and the Democratic Left, but they faced strong anti-austerity opposition from a party with a radical programme. Moreover, among the under-50s, in the larger towns and cities, and in working-class and lower-middle-class areas, SYRIZA was the leading party (Mavris, 2012). This was not a return to two-party politics, but to a politics of class where people were being offered distinctly identifiable rival programmes and visions, both for their own country and for Europe as a whole.

In retrospect, one can always find harbingers of any surprising result. Since 2010, opinion polls had consistently shown that people, often over a third of the population, considered SYRIZA as the party offering the best opposition to the successive austerity governments. They also showed that SYRIZA was gaining ground among young people under the age of 24. Inadvertently, the austerity governments, and their vocal supporters in the establishment media, especially television, may also have contributed to SYRIZA's rise. By attacking SYRIZA, and claiming to see its hand behind all forms of protest, the party gained added kudos as the most serious source of opposition. More important than this, however, was SYRIZA's actual support of such movements, irrespective of whether it had been instrumental in initiating them.

This too is not surprising. SYRIZA stemmed from a meeting of various leftist traditions, mostly communist in origin (orthodox, Eurocommunist, Trotskyist and Maoist).[113] Nearly all these had been influenced by the alter-global and anti-war movements after the turn of the century, both with respect to the ends and means of leftist politics. Synaspismos, by far the largest of the parties involved, which had its origin in the various splits of the Communist Party after 1968, perhaps underwent the greatest change of all. In the 1990s it had flirted with a strategy of progressive modernization and seemed to be sharing the trajectory of the Democratic Party in Italy towards some form of social democracy. But its increasing engagement with the European Social Forum, and its support for Left unity to overcome the divisions of the past, provided the basis for a leftwards trajectory in which leftist Eurocommunist ideas played an increasingly significant part. By its fourth Congress in 2004, this left turn was sealed by the dominance of a Left Current, and the smaller Red-Green Network, which had supported the Forum for Left Dialogue and Action out of which SYRIZA had sprung.

Therefore, SYRIZA was movement-orientated well before the Greek crisis started in earnest in 2010. Indeed, an inkling of what was to follow came after the successful education movement that had managed to block a repeal of Article 16 of the constitution in order to allow private universities.[114] SYRIZA's poll-rating soared to the high teens, almost catching that of PASOK. But this first eruption of support proved short-lived. Synaspismos' support for the December events, the split in the party over that and the left turn in general,[115] as well as party wrangling with no evident cause and differences over tactics, let alone strategy, meant that in the elections of 2009 SYRIZA's result was disappointing to say the least.

The two elections of 2012 were to prove very different. By the spring of that year Alexis Tsipras, SYRIZA's young and charismatic leader, could credibly announce that the Left was seeking to form the next government. This seemed to be the catalyst for the extraordinary events that followed. The call for a government of the Left put enormous pressure on both the KKE and the extra-parliamentary Left. For it seemed churlish, given the size of the humanitarian crisis described in Chapter 4, not to respond to an invitation which could start to bring things around. To be sure, strategic differences remained (as we shall see in Chapter 6), but to most people clutching in the wind for something to hope for, the call for unity, and one with some hope of concrete results no less, proved irresistible.[116]

The move gave focus for the tens of thousands who had been actively involved in opposing austerity measures only to see one package of cuts, or one set of 'structural' reforms, be passed after another. Suddenly, it seemed possible that these movements could be given some hope of a sympathetic government determined to change course. One that would seek not just to end the politics of austerity, but to restore the belief that democratic politics could actually change peoples' lives, while at the same time challenging the consumption and production prototypes of the neoliberal era.

Such an expanded agenda had been central to Synaspismos and SYRIZA's programmatic documents since 2009.[117] But its credibility had been boosted by exactly those movements that SYRIZA had actively supported and engaged with and the KKE had shunned. Such cross-fertilization also spread to the means of politics – the organizational structures, forms of activism, and so on. For instance, the experience of the town square influenced SYRIZA's approach to the two elections. Mass rallies, and a concentration on the mainstream media, were regulated to second place. The focus was on popular assembles in towns and neighbourhoods where the roots of the crisis and possible exits were actively discussed by unprecedentedly large numbers. Unsurprisingly, the tactics and strategy for such an exit were hotly contested, and SYRIZA's success cannot be isolated from the content of its strategy and its policy proposals (see Chapter 6).

By the end of 2012 there was, in Greece at least, a return to the kind of politics not seen since the dawn of the neoliberal era. The feeling was that countries such as Spain and Portugal were following suit. The Greek people were split down class lines. Their resistance had led to the collapse of the political centre with the spectacular demise of PASOK, which had little hope of reconnecting to its old social base. The coalition government was dominated by an increasingly authoritarian right, in both inclination and content. But the size of the recession and humanitarian crisis, as well as the scale of the fight back of the underdogs, meant that it too was unable to thread a narrative capable of consoling many of those who had once formed the backbone of the popular right. As a result the neo-Nazi Golden Dawn and the splinter populist right Independent Greeks had made significant inroads amongst New Democracy's social base. SYRIZA seemed to have consolidated its presence amongst the young, the city dwellers and the lower classes. But it was not clear whether it could breach out from such a citadel to attempt the first serious break with the neoliberal order anywhere in Europe.

6
Out of the Mire:
Arguments within the Greek Left[118]

By the end of 2012 it became increasingly clear that the latest crisis of capitalism could rival those of the 1970s and the interwar period. Within the Eurozone, Germany's more explicit commitment to preserving the euro intact, Draghi's announcement that the ECB would undertake *unlimited* bond buying ('outright monetary transactions') to help Spain and Italy, as well as the perseverance of many countries with policies of austerity and 'structural reforms', seemed to have affected expectations in a more favourable direction.

Interest rate spreads fell sharply, and there was some upgrading of economies by the rating organizations. On the other hand, most economies in the Eurozone were facing new episodes of recession or stagnation, with peripheral recession bleeding into the core; fiscal targets were not being met, and there was no end in sight to mass unemployment. Any stabilization seemed exceptionally fragile and vulnerable to various foreseeable and unforeseeable forces that could cause derailment. Not least of these was the question of whether the populations, especially in the South, would be forever willing to knuckle down and accept seemingly endless austerity and the prospect of years of economic stagnation.[119]

Elites within the Eurozone seemed unwilling to confront some of the central issues raised by the crisis: the role of the financial system, acute social inequalities, regional inequalities and the inadequacy of the economic and financial architecture. Nor was such burying of heads in the sand an exclusively European affair. Even in Obama's America, the nature of the recovery was replicating some of the worst features of the neoliberal era. Thus, Emmanuel Saez of the University of California estimated that in the recovery up to 2012, the top 1 per cent of households saw their income increase by over 10 per cent, while the bottom 99 per cent had to share a 0.2 per cent increase; while Bloomberg reported that in 2012 the 100 richest individuals had seen their wealth increase by €241 billion. *Plus ça change, plus c'est la même chose.*

Post-2008 developments underline the importance of our 'capitalist crisis' and 'lack of plasticity' theses with which we started this book. Within the EU, Angela Merkel's conservative federal vision of binding fiscal rules and a permanent Damoclean sword of competitiveness hanging over each and every economy provides the anchor of the lack of plasticity. That the EU in early 2013 could agree for the first time in its history, in a time of stagnation and widening regional divergences, to actually reduce its paltry budget is just one instance of this general phenomenon. The ability of successive Greek austerity governments to withstand all forms of resistance is another.

Perhaps a proviso is in order here with respect to our 'non-exceptionality' of Greece thesis. What is exceptional in the Greek case, and contrary to the whole drift of what we have called the 'dominant narrative', is the ability of the ruling class to preserve its privileges over time and during all phases of capitalist development. Greek society started off in 1974 as one of the poorest and most unequal in Europe, and modernizing governments managed to preserve this 'distinction' throughout the pre-crisis period. As we saw in Chapter 4, the adjustment programmes have raised inequality and poverty to new heights.

The cornerstone of these 'achievements' has been, again contrary to the dominant narrative, the remarkable prowess of ruling groups to marginalize popular and democratic elements within society; with post-crisis developments merely reinforcing this longstanding trend. The government of Antonis Samaras sought, after the summer of 2012, to merge neoliberal economics and hard-right politics. The latter included a nationalistic and anti-immigrant agenda, as well as the traditional bulwarks of Greek right-wing politics: law and order, family and the church. The first of these has been promoted with scarcely a murmur of dissent from those elements in the dominant narrative that claim some adherence to social liberalism. Moreover, the rightwards drift, far from marginalizing the neo-fascists of the Golden Dawn, has worked to legitimize their anti-immigrant and law and order agenda. New Democracy lacks a narrative to appeal to its traditional electoral base on social issues.

This makes the government vulnerable politically, especially since its centrist allies PASOK and the Democratic Left are, if anything, in an even worse position to reconnect to their traditional electoral base. The collapse of PASOK is the most significant phenomenon here. It is, of course, part of a wider trend in centre-left politics, as evidenced in François Hollande's unprecedented loss of support after his election to the French presidency, or the fact that the decline in support for the Popular Party in Spain no longer automatically translates into an equivalent rise for the party of the centre-left. As we have argued, this crisis of the political centre is one of social representation. It is difficult to envisage how this will be turned around without an agenda from centrist parties on wages, pensions and the welfare state.

Thus we return to our 'no turning back' thesis. The austerity governments in Greece have promoted a set of changes that go well beyond the neoliberal settlement. There is no indication that European elites have any concern about this trend: how it damages Europe's supposedly different social and democratic model of capitalism, and the degree of authoritarianism that has been necessary to impose such changes. Rather, Greece has been seen as a test case for the limits of the desired direction for the Eurozone as a whole. In this light, one exit from the crisis seems to be a far more authoritarian version of neoliberalism. But the crisis has also renewed interest in the possibility of a different path out of the mire.

With authoritarian politics on the rise, and centrist ones marginalized, the interest in progressive alternatives has risen. Greece has become not only the crucible of resistance and the rise of the Left – it has also seen a wide-ranging debate amongst leftists about the appropriate response to the crisis in Greece and the Eurozone as a whole. This debate has opened up nearly all the issues of a socialist strategy: from the feasibility of national roads to socialism to the nature of leftist alternatives for the economy, from the sources of capitalist ideological hegemony to class strategies for changing the balance of forces. Thus, the lessons from the debate are of interest not only to the wider Left, but to all those seeking to consider alternatives to neoliberalism.

THE GREEK LEFT AND THE EURO

One section of the Greek Left converged on a strategy of debt default and exiting the euro, together with restructuring the economy through devaluation, nationalization of the banks and the renationalization of public utilities, industrial policies etc. At the intellectual level, this approach gained support from a number of Greek academics working abroad. At the political level, it was promoted as a central policy plank by the extra-parliamentary left, especially ANTARSYA, but also found a strong, albeit minority, support within some sections of SYRIZA (see Kouvelakis, 2011:

30).[120] The exit strategy has two main elements. The first relies on a deconstruction of the argument that the EU provides a privileged terrain for left-wing strategies. The second relies on showing how debt default and euro exit provide the indispensable starting point for such strategies. It is the very cost of debt default, apparently, that will provide an inner dynamic, making (in quick succession) monetary policy independence, capital controls, nationalizations and industrial policies seem indispensable for national survival. Left-wing politics would return through this 'monetary road to socialism'.[121]

Thus, the first report published in 2010 from the Research in Money and Finance Group, based at SOAS in London, argued that the 'good euro' option (for instance introducing eurobonds, enlarging the EU budget to include larger fiscal transfers between states, or transforming the ECB into a lender of last resort) was politically infeasible (Lapavitsas et al., 2010). Europeanists, whether 'reluctant' or 'revolutionary', Lapavitsas argued, are widely overoptimistic at what can be achieved on the supranational level. Why should 'the main powers' accept major losses from a fundamental restructuring of debt at the EU level (2012: 292)? Is it surprising that the 'Eurozone establishment' has given short shrift to proposals for direct ECB financing of public debt (ibid: 293)? Moreover, is it likely that we could arrive at a coordinated European-level response to macroeconomic imbalances? After all

> There is no capitalist class that would systematically aim at raising the wages of its own workers since it would then be ruined in competition. If wage restraint was broken in Germany, the monetary union would become a lot less attractive to the German ruling class, raising the issue of its own continued euro membership. (ibid: 294–5).

It is difficult to know what to make of this form of argumentation. For there was in fact no Left in Greece arguing that the 'main powers' and the 'Eurozone establishment' would willingly accept either debt restructuring or monetary financing of public debt; nor that it is somehow in the interests of German capital to increase the wages of their workers. The whole of the Greek Left was fully aware that German capital is committed to the euro as a hard currency whose credibility is crucial to providing the framework for capital accumulation.[122] A radical strategy for the Left that gives more weight to the European-wide level is just as likely to point to the need for a fundamental shift in the balance of class forces. This was certainly the case with SYRIZA's policy that rejected the euro exit strategy.

The grounds for such a rejection were both tactical and strategic. Greece had every interest in internationalizing the problem of debt. The governments of austerity presented a simple dilemma to the Greek electorate: either accept the demands of our creditors (while hoping that negotiations can mitigate some of the worst 'excesses' of the adjustment programmes) and remain within the Eurozone, or face 'Grexit' and the extreme social costs that accompany any disorderly default. The euro exit strategy accepted the terms of this dilemma. The alternative was to challenge these terms: by pointing out that something far more systemic was at stake than a mere debt crisis; and that the debt aspects of the crisis constituted a Eurozone-wide problem best addressed at the supranational level. Such a response could appeal to the forces of labour in the South, in the first instance, but also to those in the North as well.

By the two elections of 2012, SYRIZA had come up with an electoral programme, not without a great deal of internal debate and conflict to be sure, that built on these considerations.[123] The economic aspects of the programme focused on overcoming austerity and debt, the reconstruction of the productive base of the economy and the need to reform the state.

The supporters of austerity, within and outside Greece, argued that the loans provided were integrally tied to the conditionality terms of the creditors. Politically they were of course, but analytically the integral nature of the connection depended on two assumptions: that Greece had no bargaining power with which to change the fundamental terms of the adjustment programmes, and that there was no credible alternative strategy to stabilize the economy. By the autumn of 2012 both assumptions seemed to have been undermined by events.

SYRIZA had argued from the beginning that it was extremely difficult for Greece to be thrown out of the Eurozone because a Grexit would soon lead to expectations of other departures. As was repeatedly pointed out by many economists and economic analysts, the departure of one economy violates the supposedly irrevocable commitment in a monetary union not to devalue. If one economy does nevertheless effectively devalue (through its exit), monetary union has, in effect, been transformed into a fixed-exchange-rate system. All the evidence from economic history is that such systems are extremely vulnerable in times of recession. By the summer of

2012, even Germany seemed to have come around to the idea that the systemic vulnerability of the euro made Grexit both risky and prohibitively expensive.

At the same time, the recognition that the IMF, and others, had seriously underestimated the size of the multiplier (discussed in Chapter 4) in times of recession undermined the second assumption. One report suggested that if Southern economies had implemented only half of the austerity measures actually taken, in 2012 Greece would have had 300,000 more people employed, a 6 per cent rather than a 20 per cent decline in income, and all this with the budget deficit only 1.2 percentage points higher.[124] Such findings supported the widespread feeling that much of the suffering in the South was unnecessary, thereby undermining the argument that there was only one path to economic stabilization.[125]

This all added enhanced credibility to SYRIZA's call for an international conference to provide a more just, and economically more effective, solution to the problem of Greek debt. Moreover SYRIZA was able to strengthen its hand by making explicit reference to the deal Germany achieved in the 1953 London Debt Agreement. Germany at that time had gained debt restructuring, a boost to investment from the Marshall Plan, and an agreement to pay back debt according to growth and export performance. The difference with the agreements reached between Greece and *its* creditors could hardly have been starker. The advantage of SYRIZA's strategy was that it could build on a feeling that what's good for the goose must be good for the gander.[126] Moreover, it was one that engaged with the structural problems of the Eurozone, and which could credibly claim was good not just for Greece but for the whole of the Eurozone.

SYRIZA also developed a strategy for economic development and transforming the state which, if implemented, would entail not just the end of neoliberalism, but also a significant transformation to a different kind of economy and polity. If SYRIZA's macroeconomic stance seemed to draw much from the criticisms levelled at the Eurozone by Keynesian-orientated economists, such as Paul Krugman, its microeconomics were closer to Ha-Joon Chang's (2002) attempt to rehabilitate state intervention in the economy through industrial policy, state investment banks, directed credit and so on. But there was a difference. Chang (2011), like Keynes in an earlier period, claimed to be aiming to save capitalism from itself.

SYRIZA's analysis could hardly be more different. The nature of the crisis was such that only certain social forces could take up the challenge to transcend the neoliberal economic and political order; to mobilize large sections of society to face the opposition that would surely follow from any such enterprise. It is for this reason that the Left could not just rely on 'Keynes plus more state intervention'. It had to build on the experience of those social movements that had opposed neoliberalism before and after the crisis, while making clear that its strategy did not rely on returning to some more intervention-ist, but equally statist and authoritarian, past. The phenomenon of the squares, discussed in Chapter 5, had brought to the fore the question of democracy and the return of the demos. SYRIZA was aware that the success of its strategy would stand or fall on its ability to transform this desire for participatory solutions, in the economy as well as within the state, into practical politics.

Thus, the debate of the Left was about much more than the question of the appropriate exchange-rate regime for a Left alternative. The issues raised covered some of the most basic questions faced by the Left since its conception. Three of these deserve more detailed attention.

THE NATION AND THE DEMOS

> The European Monetary Union (EMU) has created a split between core and periphery, and relations between the two are hierarchical and discriminatory. The periphery has lost competitiveness in the 2000s, therefore developing current account deficits with the core and accumulating large debts to the financial institutions of the core. The result has been that Germany has emerged as the economic master of the Eurozone. Lapavitsas et al. (2010: 5 ff.)

It is difficult not to hear echoes of the centre–periphery approach among most of the proponents of exit. In terms of practical politics, it was often difficult not to personify the enemy as Merkel and Germany, and the Troika did resemble a modern-day occupation in many aspects. But there was much more than loose talk going on here. As the above extract suggests, the main contradiction for many in the exit camp was that between the North and the South. It is one thing to analyse the macroeconomic imbalances of the Eurozone in terms of its economic and financial architecture. But it is quite another to see the Eurozone as an area for the exploitation of the countries of the periphery by the economic 'steam engine' of the centre.

Such an approach displaces a major element of Marx's problematic, namely class struggle as the motive force of historical evolution, in favour of a theoretical schema according to which contradictions and exploitative relations between capitalist social formations move history. The economic development of capitalism, and its crises, does not depend on the 'desire' or the 'strategies' of powerful states, but on the class struggle as reproduced within the links between various national states in the global economic and political order, which through their interarticulation comprise what may be described as the *global imperialist chain* (Milios and Sotiropoulos 2009: chapter 10). The imperialist chain provides, on the one hand, the locus of different (often contradictory) national strategies that are patently unequal in strength. But at the same time the unequal links in the imperialist chain have a common strategic interest: *reproduction of the capitalist system of power*. Each state, as it forges its own strategy in the international arena, also contributes to the reproduction of capitalism at the global level.

The EU comprises the integration of *capitalistically developed* European countries: a strategic coalition of their ruling classes, seeking to strengthen their position both against the US and other developed capitalist formations and, primarily, against their 'own' working classes. The key prerequisite for unimpeded capital accumulation is that there should be favourable conditions for the valorization of capital, and capitalist competition is to be included among such conditions. Exposure to international competition is the most appropriate strategy for organizing bourgeois power, as a model for the continuing reorganization of labour and the elimination of non-competitive individual capitals to the benefit of overall social capital.

Political supporters of the exit strategy somehow consider that it is a telling point, in their favour, that the EU is a powerful and authoritarian construction furthering capitalist interests, something which is not in doubt. What the debate is really about is whether this construction is primarily in order to satisfy the interests of the Northern economies. The exposure to international competition, effected through the single market programme and monetary union, imposed significant restructuring to the benefit of capital in *all* member states. Significantly, this integration secured higher rates of profit, satisfactory rates of growth and a rise in average productivity for the less competitive countries, and, before 2008 at least, went a long way towards closing the gap in per capita GDP that separated them from the more advanced countries of the European North.

In Chapter 2 we saw the extent to which Greek capital had gained from the above process. But Greek capital is not just made up of a few large banks and firms as in the folklore of state-monopoly-capital theorizing. It created, before 2008, a historic bloc on the basis of its material interests, its hegemony in ideological matters and its diverse social alliances. In the period after the crisis, as Rylmon (2011) argues:

> [the] higher social groups as well as a large section of the middle strata accept the deterioration in inequality with respect to income and social services, as they do the increase in unemployment and the spread of poverty. In spite of the fact that the consequences of the crisis, and the policies that have managed that crisis, have some effect for nearly all the population, the deterioration that has been enforced by these policies has been met with enthusiasm by a large majority of the privileged ... therefore calls for national unity in these conditions represent a failure to look at the real issue.

The 'centre–periphery' mindset, on the other hand, suggests that Greek capitalism is relatively weak: it is as if the people have a common interest against large capital, thereby considerably simplifying the problems of popular and state power. The central issue revolves around whether the basic contradiction is between capital and labour, or between capital and the 'people'. Austerity has seriously worsened the conditions of labour. The equality of insecurity, to use a telling phrase of John Gray, being imposed on both public and private sector workers has undoubtedly unified the experience of large numbers of people, and has put severe limits on individualistic responses while leading to the proletarization of sections of the middle class. What we are witnessing is the return of the social question, and the prioritization of the issues of jobs and wages. To put a radical redistribution of income at the heart of the Left's response does not limit the Left's strategy to 'a simple rejection of austerity'.[127] It merely calls for a greater degree of explicitness from possible friends and foes than the supporters of the exit strategy are willing to express.

What is needed is a discourse that elevates class, and not the 'popular', and which has the potential to unite the blue-collar worker, the precariously employed and the supermarket employee. This does not imply that there are no middle classes that can take the side of labour. But thinking about this issue relies on going beyond the anti-monopoly schemas that have dominated some parts of the Greek Left. The category of the middle classes, including the petit bourgeoisie (Milios and Economakis, 2011), covers a wide range of experiences and social practices. The Left needs to analyse these distinctions. It also needs a hegemonic politics that seeks to reach out to some these classes, not on the basis of their traditional mode of operation, which in the Greek case could simply imply tax evasion or exploiting immigrants, but on the basis of new practices and new consumption and production prototypes.

A wider social alliance, on the basis of a new hegemonic politics, can to a certain extent appeal to patriotic elements in society. Like elsewhere in Southern Europe, the Right in Greece has not been able to have such a monopoly on the patriotic card as is often the case in Northern countries. Greece's wartime resistance was predominantly organized by the Left, and the experience of a national liberalization struggle still resonates strongly.[128] But without class and ideological anchors, history suggests that such patriotic elements can be easily encompassed by the forces of nationalism.

The 'debt default and euro exit' option was adopted by a wide range of nationalistic forces, whose anti-imperialist rhetoric was not always easily distinguishable from that of certain sections of the Left.[129] The nationalistic currents mobilized around such slogans as 'Greece does not owe anything, it is owed' and 'end the foreign occupation'; both statements that resonate powerfully in a country that has not forgotten its wartime experience and all that followed. But this line of reasoning, needless to say, does not allow for any internal division between the 'people' and the 'nation'.

SYRIZA's stance with respect to the exit strategy had nothing to do with seeking a 'role of passive repositories for popular rage' (Kouvelakis, 2011: 31), but more with a class analysis of the capitalist crisis and a historical understanding of the dynamics and dangers of nationalistic politics.

DEBATING EUROPE

We have argued that the modernizers within Greece did not really have a European strategy. Rather, they had a national strategy within Europe. But the same could also be said for the Greek Left. In the post-1974 period, the Left was concerned with the restructuring of the national economy. PASOK and the KKE thought that this could be done best outside the (then) European Economic Community (EEC), while the KKE-interior, reflecting the Eurocommunist tendency within Greece, argued that a *national* strategy inside the

EEC was more viable. What was lacking from this conflict, which has subsequently re-emerged in different guises a number of times, was a strategy based *in part* on supranational solutions.

And yet the failures of the Alternative Economic Strategy in the UK, the Common Programme of the Left in France, and indeed PASOK's failure in the 1980s, all suggest that such supranational solutions are critical to left-wing political strategies. It is no accident that all three approaches were shipwrecked on the shores of finance, with financial crises in, respectively, 1976, 1983 and 1985. It is not clear that any economy, let alone one the size of Greece, can take on the financial markets. But the same could be said with respect to a number of other areas: MNCs and their ability to play one economy against the other to ensure the most favourable terms for FDI; tax competition and the ease with which the rich and the powerful can avoid paying tax through the use of tax havens; and ecological degradation and environmental regulation.

Supranational cooperation may be of equal importance for providing space for democracy. The process of European integration, as we have seen in Chapter 3, privileged economics over politics, with significant consequences not only for the quality of democratic decision making within the EU, but also for support of EU institutions amongst the peoples of Europe. Influential European public intellectuals, such as Jürgen Habermas, have in the past fought for the creation of 'public spaces' to accompany, and to counterbalance, the common market and monetary union. Habermas was particularly critical of Europe's experiments with constitution-making, especially with respect to the Treaty of Lisbon, but has more recently withdrawn to a more conservative stance (Anderson, 2012), perhaps fearing that mass mobilization in current circumstances can only mean a return of nationalistic and populist currents. Other public intellectuals, such as Etienne Balibar (2012), have, by contrast, insisted that the fight for democracy and against nationalisms within Europe must be based on popular mobilization; no less than the creation of a European people is called for if the hollowing out of democracy is to be reversed. SYRIZA's strategy, which aimed to appeal to labour in both the South and the North, was an attempt to reconnect the Left with such a democratic aspiration.

So one issue is the need for shared sovereignty in order to provide space for democratic forces. It is not at all clear that returning some functions to the nation state will result in greater autonomy for democratic and alternative initiatives. It is not as if after the crisis economies with their own currency were able to withstand the pressures of financial markets. The UK perhaps provides the paradigm case, where austerity was imposed even though it had access to an independent monetary process. The 'no alternative' in the face of the rating agencies was as likely to be heard in London as in Athens. It is not at all clear why the Left, which in the dark years of neoliberalism argued against TINA ('there is no alternative'), should discover that such a principle does, nevertheless, hold at the EU level. Elites within the EU were more than capable of bending the rules when this suited them – the 'no bailout clause' and the ban on monetary financing of debt were both quickly forgotten as the Eurozone crisis developed.[130] The bottom line is always the balance of class power.

Thus, the other issue has to do with labour's need to form alliances across national boundaries. Those arguing against the exit strategy were primarily concerned with the latter issue. The break envisaged by SYRIZA's programme was such that it was unlikely that a government of the Left would survive without a great deal of international solidarity. SYRIZA's attempt to internationalize the problem of debt and to seek a new economic and financial architecture for the Eurozone must be seen in this light. But SYRIZA had to tread a fine line. On the one hand, it needed to reject the TINA argument; that the EU was unreformable. On the one hand, it had to counter the kind of Europeanism that supported ever-greater integration, irrespective of the content of that integration and the balance of forces supporting that content.[131] In this sense it sided with Balibar contra the later Habermas.

Some in the exit camp have been keen to place their approach within the tradition of leftist internationalism. Thus it has sometimes been argued that Greece represents the weakest link in the capitalist chain, and that a radical break with the Eurozone in Greece will lead to radicalizing initiatives elsewhere. But the argument that a strategy reliant, in its initial stages at least, on a competitive devaluation to promote the competitiveness of the Greek economy can be sold as an exercise in internationalism is not particularly convincing. Moreover, the emphasis on the national economy does not suggest that an integral aspect of the strategy is the process of bringing together the largest possible concentration of the forces of labour to take on the class enemy.

CHALLENGING CAPITALIST HEGEMONY

The arguments within the Greek Left also brought to the fore a different set of issues to do with the means of politics and the nature of the socialist project. Supporters of the exit strategy gave great weight to developing the immediate political platform which would be able to radicalize the Greek population and prepare them for the implementation of that platform. Correspondingly less weight was placed on the subjects and nature of the proposed alternative. It is as if the Left has always known the path to socialism, including the optimum economic interventions along that path, and all that is needed is the appropriate political climate to reactivate the given formula. Those who recall the experience of the Alternative Economic Strategy in Britain, or the Common Programme of the Left in France, might be tempted to express some mild surprise that so little has changed with respect to the details of the economic alternative in the rather extensive intervening period.

The 'left turn' in Synaspismos in the early 2000s, which as we saw in the previous chapter was crucial to SYRIZA's dynamic rise after the crisis, had been forged in debates with the right wing of the party on the issue of 'governmentalism'. In essence, the Left within the party criticized the Right for concentrating too much time and effort on working out an appropriate programme in order to win governmental power, either alone or within a progressive coalition. The cost of such an approach was that less emphasis was given to supporting social movements that could eventually contribute to shifting the balance of power leftwards, and failing to learn from those movements about the nature of the alternative.

In short, left strategies need to build on the experience of the labour, feminist, anti-racist and other movements such as those struggling against the commodification of social and public goods. The experience of the alter-globalization movement, given its prevalence in the lean years of neoliberal hegemony, would seem to provide an excellent workshop for leftists seeking guidance about how to think about alternative economic and political strategies. Grassroots activism, self-organization, self-management, the social economy, social auditing, fair trading and ethical banking would seem to be just some of the experiences that have sprung up across the world which could realistically form the elements of a new approach. Not necessarily as alternatives to, say, democratic planning or industrial policy, but at the very least as indispensable compliments.

There are at least two common themes to many of these innovations: social needs as an essential starting point (see Lebowitz, 2003),[132] and an active response from the agents of change in addressing those needs (Laskos and Tsakalotos, 2012). But these two do not only challenge the governmentalism of the Greek Left, but also a longstanding tradition of statism and economism. It is not that the state is not an indispensable instrument for economic development. The danger lies, instead, in expecting the state to be the locus of all activity for social transformation, while at the same time downgrading the need for the state itself to be transformed with new forms of enhanced social control. Equally dangerous is elevating the issue of increasing the productive potential of the national economy above any concern about transforming the social relations of production.

For SYRIZA, proponents of the exit strategy were insufficiently vigilant with respect to both dangers. In particular, the euro exit strategy, by conflating the Left's alternative with a competitive devaluation, failed to engage with one of neoliberalism's strongest ideological cards. Breaking with the 'competitiveness' stranglehold would seem to be a priority for any left alternative. The connecting threads need to challenge both production and consumption prototypes of capitalism, and not just of the neoliberal variety; to bring to the fore, in new and interesting ways, the traditional Marxist problematic concerning who produces what for whom and how; to open up the question of new technologies and how these can serve communities rather than capitalist control over production and distribution processes; to relate directly to ecological concerns about sustainable development, or feminist concerns about the role of 'care' in our societies.

Significantly, in Greece, and especially after 2010, social resistance to austerity included diverse forms of solidarity and initiatives to set up a parallel social economy: from social clinics and pharmacies to social groceries, and from the movement to cut out the intermediaries in agricultural production to various cooperative ventures. It could be argued that these experiments were hesitant and sporadic, and that they lacked the critical mass necessary to provide viable alternative modes of consumption and production, let alone to seriously challenge the system. But it would be a mistake to see them only as expressions of solidarity with little bearing on the big picture of setting up a viable socialist economy.

Challenging capitalist hegemony requires meeting face on neoliberalism's devaluation of politics and its potential to actually change things, which we addressed in Chapter 3. Programmatic interventions can take one so far in this necessary process – if the Left is to regain its hegemony it needs to prove that it does not only say different things from the dominant elites, but also acts differently. The issue, therefore, resolves itself around the agency of social change. Thus solidarity initiatives and the social economy are better seen as practices with radical potential. At one level they provide an immediate response to the needs of those at the butt end of the neoliberal response to the crisis. But at another they provide transformative structures (Suchting, 1983), in which people come to see the value of solidarity in practice and come to see that politics, widely defined, can actually change things. To be sure, people primarily shift position because of material circumstances and ideological reconsideration. But practices that are antithetical to capitalist values can also play a key role, and the Left needs to think very seriously about the role of alternative practices.

The goal is that such a conception could affect thinking about cooperative and self-management forms, not only in the heart of the productive economy, but also within the state itself. The importance of this can hardly be overestimated. In Greece, even among progressive sections of the population, there is widespread scepticism that the existing state can be a vehicle for change in anything resembling a desired direction. This reflects not only the effects of so many years of neoliberal hegemony, but the actual workings of the Greek state – a hierarchical, inefficient, clientelistic and authoritarian state which has served Greek capitalists and their allies well. How to challenge such a state, how to democratize it, how to make it sensitive to social needs, and how to link it to forms of direct democracy, would seem to be some of the more pressing questions for the Greek Left.

CONCLUSIONS

It was not, of course, the case that the Left of SYRIZA suggested that progress towards socialism, or at least a leftist exit from the crisis, needed to wait for the resolution of such difficult questions and debates. Nor did it ever argue, as was often unfairly claimed, that change in Greece would have to wait for the simultaneous maturing of the political Left in Europe as a whole. On the contrary, as we saw in Chapter 5, it was actively involved in nearly all forms of resistance against the governments of austerity. It was clearly aware that the nation state constituted the primary locus of such resistance. But at the same time it sought to challenge traditional leftist politics by claiming that a programme of the Left never fully pre-exists independently of the movement – something which holds whether we conceive the movement towards a different society in terms of a long process of evolutionary changes within capitalism, in terms of a more condensed period of rupture with the capitalist system, or as something in between (intermediate 'ruptures' along the path to socialism as left Eurocommunists used to argue).

SYRIZA's meteoric rise during 2012 may seem to be a vindication of the position it took in the above three debates, but this would be going too far. For SYRIZA was also awarded for its commitment to left-wing unity in the face of the onslaught by austerity governments. Its appeal to both the KKE and ANTARSYA to form a common front to block existing policies had widespread resonance. It argued that the Left could unite while keeping debate on inter-left disputes open, and that the resolution to these disputes should not be posed as a prerequisite for such unity. This, more than anything, turned the tide in SYRIZA's favour in spite of, or perhaps because, its appeals fell on stony ground.

SYRIZA's recognition that it was part of something larger probably worked in its favour. The Greek Left was increasingly aware that it was facing common dangers – notably the rise of a new and far more authoritarian version of neoliberalism – and common aspirations, in terms of a progressive exit out of the mire. The scale of the crisis in Greece had led not only to the most impressive amount of resistance to authoritarian attempts to resolve the crisis, but sustained debates that sought to broach new ground. But the overall significance of both will surely ultimately depend on how this resistance, and these debates, connect to developments beyond Greece's shores.

Appendix

DOING BUSINESS IN GREECE UNDER THE MODERNIZERS

The 'Vatopedi' Scandal

Vatopedi is one of the 20 monasteries which constitute the self-governed region of Athos in northern Greece, the centre of Christian Orthodox monasticism. In September 2008, just one year after the elections when New Democracy, the conservative party, won a second term in office, a TV programme revealed one of the biggest scandals of modern Greece.

The story

Vatopedi had claimed and won – under the former, socialist government – the ownership of the third biggest lake in Greece, on the basis of property deeds dating back to the Byzantine Empire. The fact that Greece still did not have a complete land registry facilitated what was to follow. A series of land exchanges began between Vatopedi and the public authorities between 2005 and 2007. Vatopedi ended up owning several buildings worth hundreds of millions of euros, which were sold to offshore companies in Cyprus. It turned out that these offshore companies belonged to Vatopedi monks.

The people

Apart from the monks and various lawyers and businessmen that facilitated these real estate exchanges, the scandal involved many politicians and higher state officials. The most prominent included six ministers (three of whom ultimately faced judicial procedures), the director of the prime minister's cabinet and higher state officials. The church, or sections of it, had a great deal of leverage over such politicians and officials because, in national elections, the election of individual politicians depends not only on how well the party does, but also on the electorate's preference for individuals within party lists.

The consequences

From September 2008, the Vatopedi scandal was in the headlines daily and rarely off the political agenda for the next couple of years. It led to the establishment of three parliamentary committees to investigate the extent to which the ministers involved were responsible, and the temporary imprisonment of the head of the Vatopedi monastery. The seriousness of the issue was severely underestimated by the New Democracy prime minister, Kostas Karamanlis, in the autumn of 2008, during the traditional prime ministerial press conference at the Salonika Trade Fair. It was to prove a fatal error from which, it is not an exaggeration to say, he never recovered – losing the elections a year later.

The bottom line

This scandal brought to the fore what was always more than widely suspected. It was an outright manifestation of 'how-to-do-business-in-Greece'. The major political parties (New Democracy and PASOK) had always treated public funds and wealth as a means to serve particular interests. It also showed that, even in the twenty-first century, the clergy in Greece have considerable political power, underlying our analysis of how little the period of the metapolitefsi had come to grips with Greece's conservative and authoritarian past.

The SIEMENS Scandal

SIEMENS has been one of the major suppliers, if not the biggest, of the Greek state for the past decades. It has provided software, hardware, machinery and equipment in the fields of telecommunications, health, transport and defence.

The story

The scandal came to light in Greece when it became known in Germany that SIEMENS had offered bribes to politicians and other officials all over the world to gain public tenders. In Greece, a judicial investigation was launched in 2006 to examine the case, which led to the prosecution of the president, the chief executive officer and the chief financial officer of SIEMENS in Greece. However, none appeared in court, as they had fled the country. Overall, 31 people were prosecuted. A parliamentary committee of inquiry was also established in February 2010 to examine the involvement of politicians, but its conclusions shed no light on the story. The case ended in 2012 after an out-of-court settlement between the company and the Greek state.

The people

Apart from the company officials, the scandal involved numerous politicians, higher state and officials from state-owned enterprises. Only two politicians from the socialist party admitted that they had been bribed. The first, the spin doctor of former prime minister Kostas Simitis, and later an MP, admitted that in 1999 he received DM 1 million. To make matters worse, he claimed to be acting on behalf of PASOK itself and to have handed the money over to the party. The other, a former minister again from the socialist party, admitted that he was paid DM 200,000. During the time when the scandal was in the headlines, there were allegations that many politicians from the two major parties were linked to SIEMENS.

The consequences

The SIEMENS case acted as a catalyst for the future political crisis in Greece. It was a thorn in the side of both parties after the economic crisis broke out as people began to examine the reasons behind the Greek debt crisis. In short, it came to symbolize crony capitalism in Greece.

The bottom line

Not only was it suspected that large amounts of money were being passed from hand to hand, but it became clear that the political system was unable, or unwilling, to deal with it. Popular opinion held that once again those who were to blame 'got away with it'.

TIMELINE OF EUROZONE CRISIS

Date	Event	Policy
August 2007	Shortage of liquidity in money and interbank markets	ECB injects liquidity
December 2007	Shortage of liquidity continues – a number of central banks take action	ECB in joint liquidity provision with Fed ($)
17 March 2008	Bear Stearns effectively goes bankrupt – bought by JP Morgan Chase	ECB offers refinancing with six-month maturities (28 March)

July 2008		ECB increases interest rates by 25 bps
15 September 2008	Lehman Brothers files for bankruptcy	
October to December 2008		Fixed rate, full allotment refinancing, loosening of collateral rules, interest rates cut in coordinated move by 50 bps, further cut in December by 75 bps
January 2009		ECB cuts interest rates by 50 bps
March 2009		ECB cuts interest rates by 50 bps
April 2009		ECB cuts interest rates by 25 bps
May 2009		ECB cuts interest rates by 25 bps; offers one-year refinancing operations
June 2009		ECB launches the covered bond programme – buys bonds of banks and firms to help ease funding problems – up to €60 billion
December 2009		Agreement in EU to create European Banking Authority, European Insurance and Occupational Pension Authority and European Securities and Market Authority (operational from 1 January 2011)
February 2010	Greece announces a package of measures	
March 2010	EU leaders and IMF offer support to Greece	
23 April 2010	Greece seeks financial support	
2 May 2010	Support package for Greece agreed with troika	
10 May 2010		ECB launches Securities Market Programme – to purchase public and private debt securities
7 June 2010		European Financial Stability Facility established – aim is to provide loans to member states – amount available is €440 billion
30 June 2010		ECB ends covered bond purchase programme

28 July 2010		ECB tightens collateral rules
28 October 2010		EU leaders agree to strengthen the Stability and Growth Pact, and to establish a permanent crisis mechanism
21 November 2010	Ireland seeks financial support	
28 November 2010		Permanent mechanism (European Stability Mechanism) to be set up to provide financial support for member states (from mid-2013)
7 December 2010	Package agreed for Ireland with EU/IMF	
16 December 2010		Setting up of European Systemic Risk Board (response to crisis)
6 April 2011	Portugal seeks financial support	
7 April 2011		ECB raises interest rates by 25 bps
17 May 2011	Portugal's financial support package agreed	
23 June 2011		European leaders agree to increase firepower of EFSF
7 July 2011		ECB increases interest rates by 25 bps
21 July 2011		EU leaders agree to PSI – Greece an exceptional case
4 August 2011	Renewed tension in markets	ECB announces a six-month refinancing operation
August 2011	Spain and Italy commit to structural change and fiscal reform	ECB calls for EFSF to purchase government bonds in secondary market
6 October 2011		ECB announces second covered bond purchase programme – intended amount €40 billion
3 November 2011		ECB lowers interest rates by 25 bps
8 December 2011		ECB lowers interest rates by 25 bps and announces two three-year refinancing operations
9 December 2011		EU leaders agree to strengthened fiscal pact and economic policy coordination; bring forward creation of ESM to July 2012

February 2012		Loosening of collateral rules for credit claims
21 February 2012	Second adjustment programme agreed for Greece, including PSI	
28 February 2012		Greek government bonds suspended as acceptable collateral (since country in selective default)
1 March 2012		Fiscal Compact signed by EU leaders
8 March 2012		Greek government bonds accepted as collateral again (following creation of backstop)
27 June 2012	Spain and Cyrpus seek support for their banks	
29 June 2012		EU leaders agree to establish a new European supervisory mechanism for banks; ESM also given right to intervene directly in banks (not via sovereigns)
3 July 2012		ECB lowers interest rates by 25 bps – now at historic low of 75 bps
20 July 2012		ECB suspends Greek bonds as collateral (since backstop ended)
26 July 2012	Mario Draghi, President of the ECB, states that: 'Within our mandate, the ECB is ready to do whatever it takes to preserve the euro. And believe me, it will be enough'.	The statement causes spreads to narrow, especially on Spanish and Italian bonds, and stock markets rise. However, the statement is not backed up by concrete steps taken in the August meeting of the Governing Council of the ECB
6 September 2012	Governing Council of ECB announces new programme of Outright Monetary Transactions	Announcement that ECB will intervene in sovereign bond markets up to unlimited amounts provided countries have accepted conditionality and still have market access or are in the process of regaining market access
12 September 2012	German Constitu-tional Court gives green light for the establishment of the European Stability Mechanism	

26 September 2012	Spanish bond yields rise above 6% again following: (1) protests at austerity; (2) worries that Portuguese programme is going off track; and (3) news that the IMF and EC have disagreements regarding the need for more debt reduction for Greece	
28 September 2012	Official auditors' report states that Spain needs €60 billion to recapitalize its banks	Germany appears to go back on agreement of 29 June that Spanish banks will be able to be recapitalized directly through the ESM and not indirectly via the sovereign
9 October 2012	Chancellor Merkel visits Athens to meet with Prime Minister Samaras	
11 October 2012	Christine Lagarde suggests that Greece be given two more years to meet its budget commitments	
12 October 2012	Van Rompuy, President of the European Council, calls for the creation of a central treasury and budget for the euro area	
14 October 2012	Austerity protests in Portugal	
18–19 October 2012	Conclusion of European Summit	Timetable for legal framework for European single supervisory mechanism for banks clarified – to be in place by end-December. However, Chancellor Merkel announces that ESM would only be used in the future to recapitalize banks directly; it will not be used for Spanish and Italian banks now

12 November 2012	Meeting of euro area Finance Ministers	Grant Greece two more years to meet budget targets; but postpone approving disbursement of funds until 20 November as IMF and EU openly disagree on question of debt sustainability
20 November 2012	Euro area Finance Ministers meeting – again fail to reach consensus on disbursement of debt funds and measures to reduce Greek debt	
26–27 November 2012	Euro area finance ministers come to an agreement on altered adjustment programme for Greece and agree to disburse funds	Conditions attached to the agreement include Greece successfully completing a debt buy-back arrangement. Finance ministers also agree to reduce interest rates and lengthen maturities on official Greek debt. Euro area governments will also repay €7 billion in interest received on bonds held by the ECB
11 December 2012		Greece completes buy-back deal, purchasing some €32 billion of debt at a cost of €11.3 billion
13 December 2012	Meeting of Eurogroup	Agrees to disbursement of loan to Greece
14 December 2012	European Summit	Agrees to transfer banking supervision to ECB for largest banks in Europe. A mechanism for the resolution of failing banks will be put in place by end-2014
19 December 2012		ECB readmits Greek government bonds as acceptable collateral

TIMELINE OF GREEK CRISIS

9 January 2009	Standard and Poor's place Greece on negative watch (along with Ireland and then, on 12 January, Spain)
14 January 2009	Greece's rating cut by S&P from A to A–
18 March 2009	Finance minister (Papanastasiou) announces measures including public sector wage freeze to keep deficit target of 3.7% of GDP for 2009 on track
2 September 2009	Karamanlis calls elections; deficit expected to be above 7% of GDP in 2009

4 October 2009	National elections; PASOK wins outright majority
20 October 2009	Papaconstantinou announces that deficit will reach 12.5% of GDP for 2009
10 November 2009	EC reprimands Greece for its budget deficit
25 November 2009	Dubai World asks for a debt moratorium; contagion effects on Greece
8 December 2009	Fitch downgrades Greece to BBB+ with negative outlook; first time in ten years that Greece falls below A rating
14 December 2009	Papandreou announces new measures to curb deficit (cutting waste and cracking down on corruption)
17 Decembers 2009	Pharmaceutical companies claim they have not been paid arrears of €7 billion by Greek public health system
24 December 2009	Budget for 2010 passed in Parliament; forecasts deficit to GDP ratio of 9.1%(cf. 12.7% in 2009). Fiscal consolidation measures are half from expenditure side and half from the revenue side
6 January 2010	Stark (member of ECB Executive Board) states that EU will not bail Greece out
14 January 2010	Greece announces three-year plan to cut deficit to 2.8% of GDP by 2012. Growth expected to be 0.3%, 1.5% and 1.9% over the three-year period 2010–12. Markets greet announcement as too optimistic
27 January 2010	Greek bond yields and spreads at their highest level since joining euro area; MoF denies that it is selling bonds up to €25 billion of government bonds to China
28 January 2010	Prime minister and minister of finance in Davos to sell fiscal consolidation programme. EU officials state officially that they will not abandon Greece. Emergency support would come from euro area governments and not the IMF
2 February 2010	Papandreou holds emergency talks with opposition on fiscal consolidation measures
3 February 2010	EC tells Greece to cut public sector wages and improve tax collection
9 February 2010	Government announces cap on executive salaries in public sector enterprises, wage cuts for public sector workers, tax and pension reform
25 March 2010	Euro area leaders agree rescue package for Greece with participation of IMF
29 March 2010	Greece raises €5 billion through sale of seven-year bonds at interest rate of 5.9% (spread of 325 bps above German equivalent)
11 April 2010	Euro area countries agree to lend up to €30 billion to Greece in 2010 if needed; IMF likely to provide another €15 billion

23 April 2010	Greece officially requests assistance from euro area countries/IMF
2 May 2010	Euro area countries agree €110 billion package for Greece in return for cut in fiscal deficit from 13.6% of GDP to 3% by 2014
3 May 2010	ECB suspends it minimum credit rating for Greek government-backed assets used in its liquidity providing operations
10 September 2010	First review of the adjustment programme positive – 'strong start'
15 November 2010	Eurostat revises Greek budget deficit figures for previous years upwards (2010 deficit now 9.4% and not 7.8%). Greek ten-year bond yields back to levels seen before package negotiated
18 November 2010	2011 Budget goes through Parliament with additional measures of €3.5–4 billion
23 November 2010	Second review of the adjustment programme concludes that it is broadly on track
14 December 2010	Wage cuts for private and public sector workers voted in parliament to secure next tranche of bailout money
22 December 2010	Greek parliament passes budget with €14 billion of measures
30 January 2010	Greece in talks with EU and IMF to restructure debt through buyback; ECB signals its disagreement with strategy
11 February 2011	Third review of the programme ends with IMF/EC/ECB noting delays in major policy areas
15 February 2011	Economy shrunk by 4.5% in 2010
7 March 2011	Moody's reduces Greek credit rating by three notches to 'highly speculative' status
April 2011	Greek restructuring now considered inevitable
2 May 2011	Papaconstantinou announces plan to collect €11.8 billion over 2011–13 through fighting tax evasion
May 2011	Programme probably off track; debt restructuring and second programme likely required. Exit from euro area is rumoured
18 May 2011	Row surfaces over Greek restructuring between ECB, IMF and Commission
20 May 2011	Fitch downgrades Greece by several notches from BB+ to B+ and placed the country on rating watch negative
22 May 2011	Greek government fallen behind on payments to medical companies despite restructuring its debts only a few months ago
29 May 2011	IMF threatens to withhold next tranche of bailout money if financing for Athens is not secured for at least twelve months

3 June 2011	Fourth review concluded, noting progress on fiscal consolidation but need to move on structural reforms
9 June 2011	The Medium-Term Fiscal Strategy is adopted by the Cabinet and a bill submitted to parliament
17 June 2011	Venizelos replaces Papaconstantinou as finance minister
21 June 2011	Papandreou wins a vote of confidence in Parliament
24 June 2011	An extra €5.5 billion of measures needed in the four-year budget plans if targets are to be met
29 June 2011	MTFS is adopted by Parliament
3 July 2011	EU approves next release of next tranche after Greece passes measures; failure to agree to second adjustment programme
21 July 2011	Emergency summit of euro area leaders. Private sector involvement (PSI) agreed, with an average haircut of 21% in bond exchange for bonds held by the private sector. Second adjustment package agreed in principle, providing finance of €109 billion through to 2014
21 September 2011	Further spending cuts and tax increases in order to secure next tranche of finance. GDP now expected to fall by 5% (2011)
29 September 2011	New property tax paid through electricity bills passes in parliament
3 October 2011	Draft budget for 2012 presented to parliament. 2011 budget deficit revised upwards to 8. % of GDP (target 7.6%). It contains fiscal tightening of €5 billion
4 October 2011	Euro area finance ministers agree to overlook missed targets for 2011. Instead they will look at 2011–12 as a package. However, further consolidation in 2013–14 will be necessary. Moreover, the 21% haircut agreed on 21 July is likely to prove too little
11 October 2011	Fifth review mission concluded. Agreement is announced with authorities to bring programme back on track
19 October 2011	New austerity measures approved on first reading
20 October 2011	Troika approves next tranche of finance, but points to rapidly deteriorating situation. Debt to GDP ratio in particular is projected to rise to 181% in 2012 without further measures
25 October 2011	Measures passed on unified salary scale for public sector workers, the 'labour reserve', reductions in pensions, labour market reform, changes in income tax
27 October 2011	European leaders raise PSI haircut to 50%. Goal is debt to fall to 120% of GDP by 2020
31 October 2011	Papandreou calls for a referendum on the second bailout package – euro area membership
5 November 2011	Papandreou starts negotiations to form a coalition government

11 November 2011	New three-party government sworn in under leadership of Lucas Papademos. Government charged with negotiating the second adjustment programme and overseeing the completion of PSI
18 November 2011	Final budget submitted to Parliament. It sets a target of 5.4% of GDP if the debt swap is completed. It assumes a 2.8% decline in real GDP in 2012. 2011 deficit expected at 9% cf. targeted 8.5%
6 December 2011	Budget passed by parliament
10 January 2012	Omnibus bill submitted to parliament containing prior actions required to secure agreement on the second adjustment programme
31 January 2012	Omnibus bill passed – contains measures of a structural character
3 February 2012	All three leaders of the parties in the coalition reject new measures demanded by Troika in return for agreement on second adjustment programme. This leads to a delay in agreeing to the new programme at the euro-area level
12 February 2012	Measures worth €3.3 billion passed through parliament, involving pension cuts, reductions in the minimum wage and 150,000 public sector job losses
14 February 2012	Real GDP falls by 7% in 2011. Meeting of euro-area finance ministers on second adjustment programme is postponed because of disagreements between euro-area countries on whether Greece should be allowed to go bankrupt
18 February 2012	A date between 8–11 March is set for the swap of €200 billion worth of Greek debt. The swap offers bondholders 10–15% cash up front, new 30-year bonds with a coupon of 3.75% (higher if growth is faster)
21 February 2012	Agreement on second adjustment programme provided Greece passes a series of prior actions before end-February. The PSI haircut is increased from 50% to 53.5%
24 February 2012	Debt swap offer launched
1 March 2012	Finance ministers delay their approval for more than half of the second programme. The remainder will be agreed once the Greek government shows that the measures are being implemented
9 March 2012	Results of bond swap offer: 85.8% of bonds eligible were offered; with the activating of collective action clauses (CACs), the amount that will be swapped will rise to 95.7%
19 March 2012	Credit default swaps will pay out €2.5 billion on Greek bonds (21.5% of par)
11 April 2012	Elections are to be held on 6 May

6 May 2012	New Democracy are the first party with 107 seats; there follows SYRIZA with 52 seats, PASOK with 41 seats, Independent Greek with 33, KKE with 26, Golden Dawn with 21 and Democratic Left with 19. No agreement on coalition; elections called again for June 17
17 June 2012	New Democracy 129 seats; SYRIZA 71 seats, PASOK 33 seats, Independent Greek 20, Golden Dawn 18, Democratic Left 17 and KKE 12
20 June 2012	Antonis Samaras is sworn in as prime minister leading a three-party coalition of New Democracy, PASOK and the Democratic Left
20 July 2012	ECB announces Greek bonds no longer eligible as collateral in monetary policy operations
24 July 2012	Troika arrives to meet with new government
26 July 2012	Commission president Barosso visits Athens with message that reforms need to be accelerated
1 August 2012	The three-party coalition agree to €11.5 billion of cuts for the period 2013–14; PASOK drops objections to further cuts in wages and salaries
14 August 2012	€31.5 billion due to be disbursed in June now expected to be disbursed in September after Troika visit and report
14 August 2012	Greece expected to request a two-year extension to its austerity programme
25 August 2012	Hollande and Merkel reject two-year extension but reiterate their support for Greece staying in the euro area
14 September 2012	Greece's creditors hint at extension. Head of IMF states that it should be considered as an option
21 September 2012	Inconclusive talks with Troika over measures leads to rumours of a delay in disbursement of funds until November
27 September 2012	Three-party coalition agrees to new package of measures. A formal request will be made by the PM at the October EU Summit for an extension of the package to 2016
1 October 2012	Draft budget for 2013 includes measures worth €7.8 billion
31 October 2012	Revised budget for 2013 tabled in parliament. Debt-to-GDP ratio forecast to rise to 192% in 2014
7 November 2012	Parliament passes omnibus bill containing measures required to execute budget along with various prior actions
11 November 2012	Parliament passes the 2013 budget
12 November 2012	Euro area meeting of finance ministers fails to agree to release next tranche to Greece because of disagreements about debt sustainability

14 November 2012	GDP shrinks by 6.7% in the first nine months; the budget for 2013 assumes a fall of 6.5% over the whole year
18 November 2012	IMF piles pressure on EC to accept more radical measures to reduce Greece's debt to 120% of GDP by 2020
21 November 2012	Eurogroup again fails to agree on the release of some €44 billion in finance
27 November 2012	Eurogroup agrees to release of finance. Additionally, a package of measures is agreed to reduce Greece's debt burden to 124% of GDP by 2020. The package includes reductions and deferments in interest rates, lengthening of maturities, return of profits on ECB holdings of Greek bonds and a buyback scheme. Successful debt buyback necessary for release of finance
3 December 2012	Details of buyback announced. Discount on buyback expected to be between 60 and 70% of face value of bonds
13 December 2012	Buyback completed (reducing debt by €20 billion – 10% of GDP), the Eurogroup gives its approval for release of finance
19 December 2012	ECB readmits Greek government bonds as eligible collateral

Notes

INTRODUCTION

1. Our idiomatic translation of 'oloi mazi ta fagame', which literarily means 'we all ate what there was together'. The phrase implies a general tendency of consumption to exceed production capabilities, but also alludes to semi-corrupt and fully corrupt practices that contributed to Greece's deficits and debt.
2. Clientelism as a phenomenon of course goes back way before 1974. But its presence should not be interpreted as a historical given of Greek history. On the one hand its form has changed over the years: for instance, in the period after 1980 it was much more integrated into the party system. On the other hand, it has attached itself to different political and economic projects. In evolutionary, and non-functionalist, terms it has been selected by different systems to address the issue of legitimization.
3. See Crouch (2009) and Streeck (2011a) for the phenomenon of 'privatized keynesianism' and how it relates to the legitimization of capitalism.
4. Larry Summers' contention on the closeness of economics to engineering forms the starting point of Hausman and McPherson's (1996) superb book on how neoclassical economics tend to marginalize important moral issues.

CHAPTER 1

5. Later to achieve some prominence as first the Greek, and later the EU's, ombudsman. Diamandouros' work was originally published in English as a working paper, but was later republished as a book in Greek (Diamandouros, 1994).
6. It is no accident that Rostow's (1971) classic contribution on the stages of economic growth was subtitled 'A Non-communist Manifesto'.
7. See, for instance, Fernandez and Rodrik (1991).
8. Similarly, Ioakeimides (2011) would much later note the penchant of Greeks to consider themselves as being at the centre of the world.
9. The very title of Panos Kazakos' (2010) book, *From Incomplete Modernization to Crisis* encapsulates the problematic involved.
10. The legislation was eventually much watered down, but is indicative of the spirit of the times (Blyth, 2002: 134–5, 180–1).
11. See for instance, G. Voulgaris, 'Naked Power or New Collectivism', *Ta Nea,* 5 December 2009. For a critique see Laskos and Tsakalotos (2012: 85–93).
12. For an assessment of these experiments from a perspective that does not belong to the dominant narrative, see Tsakalotos (1998).
13. See his article 'Memorandum or No Memorandum: herein lies the wrong question', *Ta Nea,* 24 July 2010.
14. See G. Pagoulatos 'Insiders and Outsiders', *Kathimerini,* 27 June 2010.

15. Significantly, in Greece the original, and far more theoretically rich, critique came from the Left and not the Right. Thus early on Elephantis (1981a, 1981b) deconstructed the populist elements in PASOK's style of politics, and in particular the way it stitched together social alliances with promises that could not be delivered once governmental power had been achieved.

16. In PASOK's case, the initial hostility to European integration was radically revised in the 1980s, at least partly as a result of a growing recognition from the new socialist leadership regarding how useful EU subsidies, especially towards the agricultural sector, could be in shoring up the social alliances of the party.

17. See his article in the *Kathimerini* (9 January 2011) 'Culture and Crisis: is there an exit?' Stelios Ramfos (2011), the court philosopher of the media in Greece, was also prominent in arguing that Greek culture was responsible for defeating modernization.

18. These four features rely heavily on our reading of Harvey (2007), Amable (2010) and Crouch (2011).

19. The titles of two books, *Capitalism Unleashed* (Glyn, 2006) and *Capitalism Unbound* (Bernstein, 2010), the first by a critic, the second by a proponent, nicely capture the essence of what is at stake.

20. From this perspective it is no accident that a whole culture can be seen as an obstacle to the neoliberal exercise; something which would not have surprised Marx and Engels who, in the *Communist Manifesto,* outlined capitalism's corrosive effect on existing cultures and traditions.

21. Dyson (1999) provides an excellent account of these political debates from the mid-1990s onwards. He concludes that on the whole centre-left politicians were more in favour of interpreting the existing institutional framework flexibly than changing that framework or radically challenging the neoliberal paradigm on which it was based.

22. As was his successor to the leadership of PASOK, George Papandreou, who was fond of arguing in favour of the directive state (επιτελικό in Greek).

23. A charge favoured by Antonis Samaras, leader of New Democracy, before the two elections of 2012 that led to him forming a government of national unity (together with PASOK and the Democratic Left) in July of that year. But it was also a constant refrain of those intellectuals in Greece keen to emphasize the domestic roots of the crisis.

24. Jurgen Reinhoudt, writing approvingly in the online journal of the American Enterprise Institute, The American, 30 November 2006.

25. This time by Yiannis Vroutsis, minister of labour in Samaras' administration.

26. Much more information can be gleaned by the excellent reports of the INE/GSEE, the research institute of the Greek unions, and individual collaborators of the institute such as Yiannis Kouzis.

27. With respect to pensions, an iconic role in the modernizing narrative is the failure of the Giannitsis (the responsible minister) reform to be passed in the early 2000s.

CHAPTER 2

28. See Dragasakis (2012). The *Megali Idea,* or Grand Ideal, as a focus of national aspirations, has been a recurring theme within Greek history. The most significant, and in the end tragic, episode was the post-World War I strategy of acquiring the coastal areas of what is now western Turkey, that ended with

the 'Asia Minor catastrophe', the exchange of populations, and the end of any significant ethnic Greek presence in Ionia.

29. The question of rising wages in this period will be discussed in Chapter 3.

30. One factor in this difference is that the US and the UK can easily attract funds through international markets located in London or New York which can then be lent to domestic residents, facilitating large build-ups in debt levels and enabling the consumption aspirations of the newly emerging middle class to be realized. Germany and France, which have traditionally had more institutionally based and domestically oriented financial systems, have not been able to support the consumption desires of a new middle class to the same extent.

31. For instance, Hutton's (1996) warnings about the short-termist nature, and contradictions, of neoliberal capitalism fell on similarly deaf ears in Britain.

32. For a balanced account of the absence of social capital in Greece, see Christoforou (2005).

33. In the golden age of Greek comic cinema, roughly from the late 1950s to the early 1960s, this aspiration often forms the material for the plot. Resentment against public sector employees was to be a key factor mobilized by those supporting the first austerity package in 2010.

34. However, any explanation needs to incorporate the strategic choice of ruling groups after the end of the Civil War in 1949 in supporting such social strata as a bulwark against communism. This also explains the tolerance exhibited by the Greek state towards the self employed and small business owners in their non-payment of taxes, social security, etc. Most ruling social alliances in post-war Greece relied on their support.

35. 'Hydra or hubris', *To Vima*, 26 September 2012.

36. For modernizers such as Doxiadis (2010), any process of modernization would have needed to come to terms with the presence of small firms – incorporating them rather than wishing them away. But once more it is difficult to see what this could mean in practice, without the kind of industrial policy that modernizers tend to reject.

37. Compare tables 38B and 41B in European Commission (2012).

38. See Pizzorno (1978).

39. For an excellent critique of the public choice literature, see O'Neill (1998: chapter 12).

40. This was not how it was perceived by the dominant narrative of course. Thus Damianos Papadimitropoulos (2011), together with a number of other previous leftists, would condemn the Left in the metapolitefsi period for not breaking with the individualistic values of Greek society, and for channelling popular demands away from capital towards the state. However, this is relatively mild compared to the hatred of the metapolitefsi period, and its supposedly democratic excesses, expressed by more right-wing advocates of austerity policies after the crisis. For a critique, see Laskos and Tsakalotos (2012: 85–92).

41. The link between perceived corruption and economic performance is in fact empirically quite weak (Svensson, 2005; Shaw et al., 2011). Nor is there much warrant for claiming that economic freedom, as measured by the Heritage Foundation for instance, is correlated with enhanced economic performance (Sachs, 2005: 318–22).

42. After all, rent seeking, developed as a concept from the public choice critique of big government, should have been by now a mere memory of our more regulated and embedded past.

CHAPTER 3

43. As opposed to the more pessimistic W-shaped or L-shaped scenarios that were discussed at the time.
44. See, for different perspectives on the issue, Martin (2002), Epstein (2006), Konings and Panitch (2008) and Lapavitsas (2012a).
45. It was not a victory that went uncontested in international economic organizations such as the World Bank (Wade, 1996).
46. This difference (which is also a feature of other markets, notably labour markets) helps define, in the 'varieties of capitalism' literature, the difference between the more organized, or institutional, forms of capitalism most prevalent in Scandinavian and central European countries, and the more liberal capitalism of the Anglo-Saxon world (see Hall and Soskice, 2001).
47. See, for instance, Leo Panitch's interview with Jamie Stern-Weiner, 20 December 2012 (http://www.newleftproject.org/index.php/site/article_comments/global_capitalism_and_the_left – accessed May 2013), discussing Panitch and Gindin (2012).
48. In the early days of neoliberalism there was somewhat of a consensus that institutional divergence persevered despite the neoliberal onslaught. By the end of the period this was less easily maintained (Howell and Baccaro, 2011).
49. As Stiglitz argues (1994: 276–7), since 'whether a particular trait (species) survives depends on the environment, which is itself endogenous, there is no reason to believe that the system as a whole has any optimality properties'.
50. For a critique of the evidence on the supposed superiority of liberal finance institutions, see Zhu, Ash and Pollin (2002).
51. On the importance of tacit knowledge for socialist economies, see Gindin (1998), Devine (2002) and O'Neill (2002).
52. More detailed accounts can be found in Piketty and Saez (2003), and Duménil and Lévy (2004).
53. See, for instance, the debate in the symposium of the *Journal of Economic Perspectives* (1995) vol. 9, no. 3.
54. P. Krugman 'Graduates versus oligarchs', *New York Times*, 27 February 2006.
55. As graduates took on many of these jobs, they displaced school graduates – therefore the return to the college graduates reflects, in part, the fact that high-school graduates were earning less.
56. See Krugman (2002) and Tsakalotos (2007).
57. As envisaged by Poulantzas (1980) and his schema of integrating forms of more direct democracy with those of representative democracy.
58. Forder (2000) provides an excellent review of the evidence.
59. Meek (2012) provides a fascinating account of electricity privatization in Britain. It is a tale with many twists and turns, but one in which the public interest was rarely best served.
60. Monbiot (2001) gives a plethora of examples of such practice.
61. On both the credit crunch and the collapse of the housing bubble, see Turner (2008).

62. An accessible account of the inner workings of the financial system that led to the crisis can be found in Lanchester (2010).
63. Kindleberger (1978/2005) remains the best historical account of the processes involved.
64. In Laskos and Tsakalotos (2011: 14) we argue that, to the extent that capitalist social formations form complex wholes, monocausal explanations of crises are likely to prove unsatisfactory. Perhaps more important still, any analysis that puts at its centre class and social struggle, as the motor of history, will have to deal not only with the political and ideological moments of the crisis but also with unpredictable eventualities that are not fully determined.
65. See Thomas Frank's 'The Rise of Market Populism', *The Nation*, 30 October 2000.
66. See, for instance, his 'Why cautious reform is the risky option', *Financial Times*, 27 April 2010.
67. Whether Greece is exceptional is discussed in Chapter 4.
68. Douzinas (2011: 157–9) provides an excellent account of many aspects of this deficit, from the great mass of legislation that stems from the EU that national parliaments never discuss, to the way lobbying has replaced democratic procedures and the electoral process. Douzinas speaks in terms of the whole process resembling more the machinations of the Holy Roman Empire than that of a modern-day democracy, whereas Perry Anderson (2009: 117), on a similar medieval theme, suggests that what we have, in essence, is a return to the practice of petitioning the prince.
69. The goals set out in the Lisbon process for employment and unemployment were very far from being achieved, even before the onset of the world economic crisis in 2008 (Pisani-Ferry and Sapir, 2006; EC, 2010).
70. Note that 2007 and 2008 are shown because the timing of the impact of the crisis in euro area countries varied – since the crisis has caused a cyclical decline in the size of current account imbalances it could give a misleading impression of a structural correction of imbalances, whereas in fact it is just a cyclical phenomenon.
71. See M. Wolf 'The sad record of fiscal austerity', *Financial Times*, 26 February 2013 and Paul De Grauwe and Yuemi Ji 'Panic-driven austerity in the Eurozone and its implications', *The Vox Blog*, 21 February 2013.
72. Thus, Peter Bofinger (2012) argued not only for a change in the policies of austerity for Greece, but for important institutional changes at the EU level, such as a socialization of the debt so that interest rates do not go above 3–4 per cent and a European finance minister responsible to the European Parliament. Varoufakis and Holland (2012) provided a well thought-out alternative to dealing with the European debt problem at the supranational level.

CHAPTER 4

73. Paul A. Porter (1904–75) was a journalist and lawyer. A registered Democrat and fervent New Dealer, he arrived in Athens to head the American Mission to prepare the ground for bilateral aid to Greece – what was soon to become known as the Truman doctrine. His report was crucial in shaping future US aid policy in Greece. His critical references to the country's financial and political elites were shared by Kyriakos Varvaressos (2002/1952), a prominent economist, academic, governor of the Bank of Greece and statesman, who

is often remembered for his attempt to stabilize Greece's public finances and put an end to hyperinflation.

74. Both phrases, the first from George Papandreou and the second from George Papakonstantinou, who became minister of finance, were to haunt the PASOK government as events unfolded.

75. Most notably following Dubai World's request for a debt moratorium in November 2009.

76. As we saw in the previous chapter, for Wolfgang Schäuble anything else would have led to 'moral hazard', alleviating the incentive to fully implement the programme.

77. In terms of economic results, Monti too did little more than guarantee the safeguarding of elite privileges, emphasizing that austerity and neoliberal structural reform was the only path available. His extremely poor showing in the election of February 2013 aptly demonstrated the limits of a politics that elevated political credibility above economic and social results.

78. The Democratic Left, a recently formed party, consisted of a core that had left Synaspismos (by far the largest party in the SYRIZA coalition), and a sprinkling of support from some in PASOK that had opposed the austerity policies of their government.

79. New Democracy's opposition to austerity before the summer of 2012 was always ambiguous. On the one hand, it complained that certain structural reforms, notably privatizations, were being delayed; thereby indicating its more rigorous support for the neoliberal programme. On the other hand, it claimed that the policy mix was all wrong, and that it would introduce 'equivalent' measures when in power that would be both more just and more expansionary. Needless to say, such measures were notable by their absence once Antonis Samaras formed his government.

80. The debt swap entailed swapping government bonds with, say, a face value of €100 with bonds with a face value of less than €50. Thus, any investor with a €100 investment in Greek government bonds would ultimately receive less than half of his/her initial investment. The debt buyback was a similar transaction in the sense that investors received considerably less than initially invested. However, instead of receiving bonds worth less than €50, the investor effectively received cash (more precisely, investors received European Financial Stability Fund bonds which were easily sellable for cash).

81. Net, that is, of the money borrowed to recapitalize the banking system (some 20 per cent of GDP).

82. See Krugman (2001) for a very accessible account of various generations of models.

83. The Exchange Rate Mechanism (ERM) was an attempt to create a zone of monetary stability (i.e. low inflation) through fixing exchange rates, essentially to the deutschemark. For some, it was conceived as a stepping-stone to monetary union. However, as is often the case, fixed exchange rate systems become very vulnerable in periods of recession and high unemployment and, in the crisis of 1992 and 1993, the UK and Italy had to leave the fixed exchange rate system.

84. These models have multiple equilibria. Without fear, the outcome is the good equilibrium and the government is solvent; it is the presence of fear that causes the economy to end up in the bad default equilibrium.

85. It is true to say that Greece's debt was increasingly foreign-owned, pointing to the existence of a competitiveness problem as well as a fiscal one. But, as we saw in the previous chapter, this was not the result of particularly poor productivity performance – a large part of the responsibility lies with the economic architecture of the Eurozone.

86. PASOK modernizers would place a large part of the blame for the crisis on the second Karamanlis government (2007–9). While it is clear that some loss of fiscal control occurred, this critique is clearly an exercise aimed at obscuring their own responsibility for the vulnerability of the Greek economy. The vehemence of the conflict between PASOK and New Democracy cannot hide their underlying agreement on the fundamentals. Their eventual cooperation merely confirmed what most observers had long accepted.

87. Newspaper reports suggest figures of €9–12 billion, more than 5 per cent of GDP and twice initial estimates.

88. Initially three support packages for the banking sector were passed through parliament. The first in 2008 amounted to €28 billion, the second €15 billion (May 2010) and the third €25 billion (August 2010). These support packages created potential liabilities for the state.

89. Similar considerations apply to much larger economies such as Italy (see Michael Roberts, in his excellent Marxist economics blog, http://thenextrecession. wordpress.com/2012/12/, accessed May 2013).

90. Rajan (2012) 'Legitimacy rests on restoring opportunity', *Financial Times*, 18 October 2012.

91. Indeed, the Troika eventually refused to allow Greek governments to include revenues from reducing tax evasion into adjustment proposals. Their stance was that if these revenues miraculously materialized, then the government could be more lax in a subsequent period.

92. Government ministers were prone to compare Greece to the 'Titanic', or despair over whether enough money was available for pensions and the state health system.

93. See Wolfgang Münchau, 'Monti is not the right man to lead Italy', Financial Times, 20 January 2013.

94. Exposure of a banking sector to sovereign bonds from its country of origin is, of course, nothing exceptional.

95. Alamanou et al., 'The Configuration of Homelessness in Greece during the financial crisis', September 2011, KLIMAKA NGO. The qualitative analysis of this study shows that the homeless include ex-businessmen and higher-education graduates.

CHAPTER 5

96. Thus, as late as 1977, the McCracken Report of the OECD was predicting such a return once the policy mistakes of excessive monetary expansion had been corrected.

97. The reference to the December events, the Dekemvriana as they are referred to in Greece, is highly loaded in a Greek context. In December 1944, British troops, operating out of the Grande Bretagne hotel, opened fire with many casualties on a peaceful demonstration in Syntagma Square organized by the resistance movement. It was perhaps the opening act in Greece's civil war, which was only to end with the defeat of the Left in 1949.

98. Seferiades and Johnston (2012), an edited volume that provides many of the best accounts of the events, uses 'eruption'; the more conventional Economides and Monastriotis (2009) volume goes with 'riots'.

99. Even the *Economist* (11 December 2008) accepted that 'The feel-good factor allowed the conservatives to ignore the pressing case for social reform, particularly in education, health and policing. But as the global slowdown takes effect, young Greeks see their parents struggle to pay the bills'.

100. For a discussion of spontaneity in the December events see Dalakoglou (2012).

101. Later there would be some backsliding on the promises made, but there is no doubt that the hunger strikers had won an important victory.

102. Even the less orthodox PCI and PCF had serious trouble in coming to terms with the new social movements of the 1960s, with, as Rossana Rossanda (2010) has recently argued, serious political consequences for the European Left as a whole.

103. The 227-day strike and occupation at the steel works at Aspropirgos, just outside Athens, is a case in point. A classic confrontation of industrial workers opposing redundancies and wage cuts was supported actively by a number of leftist groups and social movements, but the response from the official labour movement was lukewarm.

104. The KKE organized its own demonstrations at different times and venues, only rarely allowing some form of contact with the main body of the protestors. It was a defensive strategy which was hardly geared to enlarging the party's base of support, let alone maximizing the effectiveness of the opposition to austerity.

105. See Branco, L. 'One of the biggest strikes ever', *International Viewpoint,* 20 November 2012.

106. The diverse set of movements here went under the banner of Won't Pay, Won't Pay, which is, in actual fact, a closer translation of Dario Fo's play than the English version.

107. Syntagma means constitution, and takes its name, significantly, from the movement in 1843 that successfully imposed a constitution on King Otto of Bavaria.

108. See Hardt and Negri (2012) and Charnock et al. (2012).

109. In the first few days Greek flags and patriotic slogans were omnipresent in Syntagma. But soon young leftists with Portuguese, Spanish, Irish, Tunisian and other flags were able to add a strong internationalist element to the proceedings.

110. The square itself was split between an upper half nearest to parliament that was more disparate in its political and social composition, and more confrontational and oppositional, where the focus was on the fall of the government and the abandonment of the adjustment programmes; and a lower half, where the Left tended to dominate, and where the daily discussion and decision-making assemblies pressed for alternative policies and a new democratic order to combine forms of direct democracy with those of the representative kind.

111. See the Political Barometer of the polling organization *Public Issues,* July 2010 (http://www.publicissue.gr/wp-content/uploads/2011/07/varometro-07-2011.pdf – accessed May 2013).

112. At the outset, some of the media was rather sympathetic to what was at first seen as a new form of anti-politics that could perhaps marginalize the Left. If so this 'mistake' perhaps gave the squares an initial boost that might otherwise

have been unavailable. The story of bias in the Greek media, and especially television, has yet to be written. During the elections of 2012 this bias took on unprecedented forms of hostility against the Left, paralleling the role of the media in some Latin American countries, where they undoubtedly form the vanguard of the ideological state apparatuses.

113. By 2011 there was a growing inflow of people from PASOK, most of which formed the United Social Front (EKM). From then on the party was officially called SYRIZA-EKM.

114. But the victory turned out to be rather pyrrhic. Soon afterwards the forward march of neoliberal reforms in education continued unabated. Educational movements have a long track record in Greece, since at least the 1960s. The lack of ultimate success in the Article 16 clash may have ultimately undermined such traditional forms of protest in favour of some of the alternatives discussed in this chapter.

115. The split led to the creation of the Democratic Left which was, after the elections of 2012, to support the pro-austerity government of Samaras.

116. The KKE and ANTARSYA, of the extra-parliamentary Left, failed to change track even between elections, when the pressing need for unity was even more obvious. The result was that in the June election the KKE's vote fell from 8.5 per cent to 4.5 per cent, while ANTARSYA's collapsed to 0.3 per cent.

117. Kouvelakis' (2011) assessment that SYRIZA's programme was limited to opposing austerity was widely off the mark.

CHAPTER 6

118. This chapter draws heavily on Laskos, Milios and Tsakalotos (2012).

119. See, for instance, Martin Wolf, 'Why the euro crisis is far from over', *Financial Times*, 19 February 2013, and Paul De Grauwe and Yuemi Ji, 'Panic-driven austerity in the Eurozone and its implications', *The Vox Blog*, 21 February 2013.

120. The KKE, as ever, remained aloof from the dispute. On the one hand, its traditionally anti-EU stance made it seem closer to a debt default and euro exit strategy. On the other hand, its class-based politics made it sceptical of raising the euro, and more generally the national question, over that of class.

121. The term belongs to Yiannis Milios.

122. We are less convinced, however, of the argument that Germany is so committed, as Lapavitsas (2012b) seems to believe, to the importance of the euro as a form of world money. Germany, before the euro, was always sceptical about the deutschmark turning into a major reserve currency, and this scepticism has carried over with respect to the euro.

123. A version in English can be found at: http://www.syn.gr/gr/keimeno.php?id=27332 (accessed May 2013).

124. See Economic Outlook, *Oxford Economics*, vol. 37, issue 1.

125. If this was in fact the goal, and not the austerity measures and structural reforms as such (see Chapters 3 and 4).

126. The economic historian Albrecht Ritschl ('Germany, Greece and the Marshall Plan', *The Economist*, 15 June 2012) shows that this comparison is far from unfair; that Germany gained far more from the London Agreement than the Marshall Plan.

127. As unfairly suggested by Kouvelakis (2011: 29).

128. Although EAM, by far the most important resistance organization, is mostly remembered for blowing up bridges and other feats against the Nazis, its organization in 1943 of mass demonstrations in Athens against political mobilization (i.e. sending Greek workers to work in Germany) is probably of even more significance. It would be a mistake to underestimate the class elements in the resistance experience.

129. Thus D. Kazakis, an independent economist, originally from the KKE, eventually set up his own party with identifiable nationalistic sentiments. Before that, his support for the default and exit option ensured that he was given a platform by leftist organizations that should have known better. Another case was that of Spitha (spark), a group that coalesced around the famous musician Mikis Theodorakis. Theodorakis is a historic figure of the Left, but his increasingly patriotic rhetoric, and some unsavoury company, meant that it was the nationalistic aspects of the Spitha that dominated. Both these initiatives fizzled away before the 2012 elections.

130. The Greek, Irish and Portuguese bailouts, and Draghi's promise for 'outright monetary operations', confirm this 'flexibility'.

131. Within Greece this was, in essence, the stance taken by the Democratic Left, which by the summer of 2012 supported the austerity government of Antonis Samaras. There is a clear line of continuity between the elitist conception of European integration supported by Monnet, discussed in Chapter 3, and the Democratic Left's support for a European project whatever the content of such a venture.

132. The 'economy of needs' formed the core of Synaspismos' 'left turn' at the programmatic level during a special conference convened to discuss its programme in 2009.

References

Amable, B. (2010) 'Morals and Politics in the Ideology of Neo-liberalism', *Socio-Economic Review*, vol. 9, pp. 3–30.

Anderson, P. (2002) 'Force and Consent', *New Left Review*, no. 17, pp. 5–30.

Anderson, P. (2009) *The New Old World*, Verso Books.

Anderson, P. (2012) 'After the Event', *New Left Review*, no. 73, pp. 49–61.

Balibar, E. (2012) 'What Democratic Europe? A Response to Jürgen Habermas', *Social Europe Journal*, 1 October.

Bernstein, A. (2010) *Capitalism Unbound: The Incontestable Moral Case for Individual Rights*, University Press of America.

Blackburn, R. (1999) 'The New Collectivism: Pension Reform, Grey Capitalism and Complex Socialism', *New Left Review*, no. I/233, Jan/Feb, pp. 3–65.

Blyth, M. (2002) *Great Transformations: Economic Ideas and Institutional Change in the Twentieth Century*, Cambridge University Press.

Bofinger, P. (2012) *Zurück zur D-Mark: Deutschland braucht den Euro*, Droemer Verlag.

Boyer, R. (2012) 'The Four Fallacies of Contemporary Austerity Policies: The Lost Keynesian Legacy', *Cambridge Journal of Economics*, vol. 36, no. 1, pp. 283–312.

Brenner, R. (2006) *The Economics of Global Turbulence*, Verso Books.

Buchanan, J. and Tullock, G. (1962) *The Calculus of Consent*, Michigan University Press.

Carr, E.H. (1961) *What is History?* Cambridge University Press.

Chang, H-J. (2002) *Kicking Away the Ladder*, Anthem Press.

Chang, H-J. (2011) *23 Things They Don't Tell You about Capitalism*, Penguin Books.

Charnock, G., Purcell, T. and Ribera-Fumaz R, (2012) '¡Indignate!: The 2011 Popular Protests and the Limits to Democracy in Spain', *Capital and Class*, vol. 36, no. 1, pp. 3–11.

Chibber, V. (2005) 'Capital Unbound', *New Left Review*, no. 36, pp. 151–8.

Christoforou, A. (2005) 'On the Determinants of Social Capital in Greece Compared to Countries of the European Union', *FEEM*, Working Paper, vol. 68.

Crouch, C. (2004) *Post-Democracy*, Polity Press.

Crouch, C. (2009) 'Privatized Keynesianism: An Unacknowledged Policy Regime', *British Journal of Politics and International Relations*, vol. 11, no. 3, pp. 382–99.

Crouch, C. (2011) *The Strange Non-Death of Neo-liberalism*, Polity Press.

Dalakoglou, D. (2012) 'Beyond Spontaneity: Crisis, Violence and Collective Action in Athens', *CITY*, vol. 16, no. 5, pp. 535–45.

De Angelis, M. (2007) *The Beginning of History: Value Struggles and Global Capital*, Pluto Press.

De Grauwe, P. (2012) 'The Governance of a Fragile Eurozone', *Australian Economic Review*, vol. 45, no. 3, pp. 255–68.

Deutsche Bank (2012) 'The Impact of Tax Systems on Economic Growth in Europe', *EU Monitor, European Integration*, October 5.

Devine, P. (2002) 'Participatory Planning through Negotiated Coordination', *Science and Society*, vol. 66, no. 1, pp. 72–85.

Diamandouros, N. (1994) *Cultural Dualism and Political Change in Post-authoritarian Greece*, Estudio/Working 1994/50, Centro de Estudios Avanzados en Ciencias Sociales, Instituto Juan March de Estudios e Investigaciones, Madrid, 1994; published in Greek as *Political Dualism and Political Change in Post-authoritarian Greece*, Alexandreia Press, 2000.

Douzinas, C. (2011) *Resistance and Philosophy in the Crisis: Greece and the Future of Europe*, Alexandreia (in Greek – English version Wiley, 2013).

Doxiadis, A. (2010) 'Households, Rentiers, Speculators', *Athens Review of Books*, no. 8, June (http://www.opendemocracy.net/aristos-doxiadis/owners-rentiers-opportunists – accessed May 2013).

Dragasakis, Y. (2012) *What Exit? From what Crisis? With which Social Forces?*, Taxideutis, (in Greek).

Duménil, G. and Lévy, D. (2004) *Capital Resurgent: Roots of the Neoliberal Revolution*, Harvard University Press.

Duménil, G. and Lévy, D. (2010) *The Crisis of Neoliberalism*, Harvard University Press.

Dyson, K. (1999) 'Benign of Malevolent Leviathan? Social Democratic Governments in a Neo-liberal Euro Area', *Political Quarterly*, vol. 79, no. 2, pp. 195–209.

EC (2010) *Lisbon Strategy Evaluation Document*, SEC (2010) 114 Final, 2 February 2010.

Economides, S. and Monastriotis, V. (eds) (2009) *The Return of Street Politics?: Essays on the December Riots in Greece*, The Hellenic Observatory, The London School of Economics and Political Science.

Eijffinger, S. (2009) 'Adjustments to the Accountability and Transparency of the European Central Bank', *VoxEU.org* (http://www.voxeu.org/article/coordinating-european-financial-supervision – accessed May 2013).

Elephantis, A. (1981a) 'PASOK and the Elections of 1977: The Rise of the Populist Movement', in Penniman H.R. (ed.) *Greece at the Polls: The National Elections of 1974 and 1977*, American Enterprise Institute, Washington DC.

Elephantis, A. (1981b) *Unfound Socialism*, Politis, (in Greek).

Epstein, G. (2006) *Financialization and the World Economy*, Edward Elgar.

European Commission (2012) *General Government Data: General Government Revenue, Expenditure, Balances and Gross Debt, Part II: Tables by Series*, European Commission, Economic and Financial Affairs, Autumn.

Fernandez, R. and Rodrik, D. (1991) 'Resistance to Reform: *Status Quo* Bias in the Presence of Individual-specific Uncertainty', *American Economic Review*, vol. 81, no. 5, pp. 1146–55.

Fine, B. (2010) 'Beyond Financialisation', unpublished mimeo.

Finlayson, A. (2010) 'The Broken Society Versus the Social Recession', *Soundings*, No. 44, Spring, pp. 22–34.

Forder, J. (2000) 'Central Bank Independence and Credibility: Is there a Shred of Evidence?: Review', *International Finance*, vol. 3, no. 1, pp. 167–85.

Frank, T. (2006) *What's the Matter with America? The resistible Rise of the American Right*, Vintage.

Freeden, M. (1999) 'The Ideology of New Labour', *Political Quarterly*, vol. 70, no. 1, pp. 42–51.

Giavazzi, F. and Pagano, M. (1988) 'The Advantage of Tying One's Hand: EMS Discipline and Central Bank Credibility', *European Economic Review*, vol. 32, no. 5, pp. 1055–75.

Gibson, H. (1989) *The Euro-Currency Markets, Domestic Financial Policy and International Instability*, Macmillan.

Gibson, H. and Tsakalotos, E. (1994) 'The Scope and Limits of Financial Liberalisation in Developing Countries: A Critical Survey', *The Journal of Development Studies*, vol. 30, no. 3, pp. 578–628.

Gibson, H. and Tsakalotos, E. (2003) 'Finance–Industry Relationships in Europe and the Prospects for Growth and Convergence', in Arestis, P., Beddeley, M. and McCombie, J. (eds), *Globalisation, Regionalism and Economic Activity*, Edward Elgar.

Giddens, A. (1998) *The Third Way*, Polity Press.

Gindin, S. (1998) 'Socialism with Sober Senses: Developing Workers' Capacities', in Panitch, L. and Leys, C. (eds), *Socialist Register 1998*, Merlin Press.

Glyn, A. (2006) *Capitalism Unleashed: Finance, Globalization, and Welfare*, Oxford University Press.

Goldthorpe, J. (1987) 'Problems of Political Economy after the Post-war Period', in Maier, C.S. (ed.), *Changing Boundaries of the Political: Essays on the Evolving Balance Between the State and Society, Public and Private in Europe*, Cambridge University Press.

Gowan, P. (1999) *The Global Gamble: Washington's Faustian Bid for World Dominance*, Verso.

Grahl, J. (2001) 'Globalised Finance: The Challenge of the Euro', *New Left Review*, no. 8, pp. 23–46.

Green, F. (2007) *Demanding Work: The Paradox of Job Quality in the Affluent Economy*, Princeton University Press.

Hall, P. and Soskice, D. (2001) *Varieties of Capitalism: The Institutional Foundations of Comparative Advantage*, Oxford University Press.

Hall, S. (2003) 'New Labour's Double-shuffle', *Soundings*, no. 24, pp. 10–24.

Hall, S. and Massey, D. (2010) 'Interpreting the Crisis', *Soundings*, no. 44, pp. 57–71.

Harrison, B. and Bluestone, B. (1988) *The Great U-turn: Corporate Restructuring and the Polarization of America*, Basic Books.

Hardt, M. and Negri, A. (2012) *Declaration*, Argo-Navis.

Harvey, D. (2007) *A Brief History of Neoliberalism*, Oxford University Press.

Harvey, D. (2010) *The Enigma of Capital*, Profile Books.

Hausman, Daniel H. and McPherson M.S. (1996) *Economic Analysis and Moral Philosophy*, Cambridge University Press.

Hecker, D. (1992) 'Reconciling Conflicting Data on Jobs for College Graduates', *Monthly Labour Review*, July, pp. 3–12.

Hirst, P. and Thompson, G. (1996) *Globalization in Question*, Polity Press.

Hodgson, G. and Jiang, S. (2007) 'The Economics of Corruption and the Corruption of Economics: An Institutionalist Perspective', *Journal of Economic Issues*, vol. XLI, no. 4, pp. 1043–61.

Holland, D. and Portes, J. (2012) 'Self-defeating Austerity?', *VoxEU.org*, (http://www.voxeu.org/article/self-defeating-austerity – accessed May 2013).

Howell, C. (2003) 'Varieties of Capitalism: And Then There Was One?', *Comparative Politics*, vol. 36, no. 1, pp. 106–24.

Howell, C. and Baccaro, L. (2011) 'A Common Neoliberal Trajectory: The Transformation of Industrial Relations in Advanced Capitalism', *Politics & Society*, vol. 39, no. 4, pp. 521–64.

Hutton, W. (1996) *The State We're In*, Vintage.

Ioakimidis, P. (2011) 'Crisis and Greek Exceptionalism', *Athens Review of Books*, no. 15, (http://www.booksreview.gr/index.php?option=com_content&view=article&id=96:-15-2011&catid=46:-15-2011&Itemid=55 – accessed May 2013).

Ioannides, G. (2012) *The Political Economy of Greek Employment Policy*, PhD, Department of Economic Science, University of Crete.

Jessop, B. (2002) *The Future of the Capitalist State*, Polity Press.

Kalecki, M. (1943) 'The Political Aspects of Full Employment', *The Political Quarterly*, vol. 14, no. 4, pp. 322–30.

Karamessini, M. (2008) 'Still a Distinctive Southern European Employment Model?', *Industrial Relations Journal*, vol. 39, no. 6, pp. 510–31.

Katz, R. and Mair, P. (2009) 'The Cartel Party Thesis: A Restatement', *Perspectives on Politics*, vol. 4, no. 4, pp. 753–66.

Kay, J. (2007) 'The Failure of Market Failure', *Prospect*, August, (http://www.prospectmagazine.co.uk/magazine/thefailureofmarketfailure/ – accessed May 2013).

Kazakos, P. (2010) *From Incomplete Modernization to Crisis: Reforms, Debt and Inertia in Greece (1993–2010)*, Patakis (in Greek).

Kindleberger C. (1978/2005) *Manias, Panics and Crashes*, Macmillan.

Konings, M. and Panitch, L. (2008) 'US Financial Power in Crisis', *Historical Materialism*, vol. 16, vol. 4, pp. 3–34.

Kouvelakis, S. (2011) 'The Greek Cauldron', *New Left Review*, no. 72, pp. 17–32.

Kouzis, G. (2007) *The Characteristics of the Greek Union Movement*, Gutenberg (In Greek).

Krugman, P. (2001) 'Crises: The Next Generation', mimeo, (http://www.princeton.edu/~pkrugman/next%20generation.pdf – accessed May 2013).

Krugman, P. (2002), 'For richer', *New York Times*, 20 October.

Krugman, P. and Wells R. (2011) 'The Busts Keep Getting Bigger: Why?', *New York Review of Books*, vol. LVIII, no. 12, pp. 28–9.

Lanchester, J. (2010) *Whoops! Why Everyone Owes Everyone and Nobody Can Pay*, Penguin Books.

Lapavitsas, C. (2012a) *Financialization in Crisis*, Haymarket Books.

Lapavitsas, C. (2012b) 'Default and Exit from the Eurozone: A Radical Left Strategy', *Socialist Register 2012: The Crisis and the Left*, vol. 48, (http://socialistregister.com/index.php/srv/issue/view/1223, accessed May 2013).

Lapavitsas, C., Kaltenbrunner, A., Lindo, D., Michell, J., Painceira, J.P., Pires, E., Powell, J., Stenfors, A. and Teles, E. (2010) *Eurozone Crisis: Beggar Thyself and Thy Neighbour*, Research on Money and Finance, Occasional Report.

Laskos, C., Milios, J. and Tsakalotos, E. (2012) 'The Greek Left and the Euro', unpublished mimeo.

Laskos, C. and Tsakalotos, E. (2011) *No Turning Back: Capitalist Crises, Social Needs, Socialism*, Ka Psi.Mi. editions, (in Greek).

Laskos, C. and Tsakalotos, E. (2012) *22 Things that they tell you about the Greek crisis that aren't so*, Ka Psi.Mi. editions, (in Greek).

Lebowitz, M. (2003) *Beyond 'Capital': Marx's Political Economy of the Working Class*, Macmillan.

Lukes, S. (1975) *Power: A Radical View*, Macmillan.

Lyberaki, A. and Tsakalotos, E. (2002) 'Reforming the Economy without Society: Social and Institutional Constraints to Economic Reform in post-1974 Greece', *New Political Economy*, vol. 7, no. 1, pp. 93–114.

Maier, C.S. and Lindberg, L.N. (1985) 'Alternatives for Future Crises', in Lindberg, L.N. and Maier, C.S. (eds), *The Politics of Inflation and Economic Stagnation*, The Brookings Institution.

Marquand, D. (2004) 'The Public Domain is a Gift of History. Now it is At Risk', *The New Statesman*, 19 January, pp. 25–8.

Martin, R. (2002) *The Financialization of Daily Life*, Temple University Press.

Massey, D. (2010) 'The Political Struggle Ahead', *Soundings*, no. 45, pp. 6–18.

Matsaganis, M. (2011) *Social Policy in Difficult Times*, Kritiki (in Greek).

Mavris, Y. (2012) 'Greece's Austerity Election', *New Left Review*, no. 76, pp. 95–107.

Mayer, C. (1994) 'The Assessment: Money and Banking: Theory and Evidence', *Oxford Review of Economic Policy*, vol. 10, no. 4, pp. 1–13.

McCormick, A., Horn, L. and Knepper, P. (1996) *A Descriptive Summary of 1992/93 Degree Recipients 1 Year Later*, US department of Education, National Center for Education, Washington DC.

Meek, J. (2012) 'How We Happened to Sell Off Our Electricity', *London Review of Books*, vol. 34, no. 17, pp. 3–12.

Milios, J. (2004) 'Does "Anti-imperialism" Constitute a Basis for Left-wing Ideology and Politics?', *Theseis*, no. 88, (in Greek) (http://www.theseis.com/index.php?option=com_content&task=category&sectionid=4&id=28&Itemid=29 – accessed May 2013).

Milios, J. and Economakis, G. (2011) 'The Middle Classes, Class Places, and Class Positions: A Critical Approach to Nicos Poulantzas's Theory', *Rethinking Marxism*, vol. 23, no. 2, pp. 226–45.

Milios, J. and Sotiropoulos, D. (2009) *Rethinking Imperialism: A Study of Capitalist Rule*, Macmillan.

Milios, J. and Sotiropoulos, D. (2011) *Imperialism, Financial Markets, Crisis*, Nisos (in Greek).

Minsky, H. (1982) *Inflation, Recession and Economic Policy*, Harvester Wheatsheaf.

Monbiot, G. (2001) *Captive State: The Corporate Takeover of Britain*, Pan Macmillan.

Mouzelis, N. (1980) 'Thoughts on the Impressive Political Rise of PASOK', in Andrianopoulos, A. et al. (eds), *PASOK and Power*, Paratiritis (in Greek).

Navarro, V. (2011) 'The Crisis and Fiscal Policies in the Peripheral Countries of the Eurozone', *Social Europe Journal*, 24 June (http://www.social-europe.eu/2011/08/the-crisis-and-fiscal-policies-in-the-peripheral-countries-of-the-eurozone/ – accessed May 2013).

Olson, M. (1965) *The Logic of Collective Action*, Harvard University Press.

O'Neill, J. (1998) *The Market: Ethics, Knowledge and Politics*, London, Routledge.

O'Neill, J. (2002) 'Socialist Calculation and Environmental Valuation: Money, Markets and Ecology', *Science and Society*, vol. 66, no. 1, pp. 137–51.

Panitch, L. and Gindin, S. (2012) *The Making of Global Capitalism*, Verso Books.

Papadatos-Anagnostopoulos D. (forthcoming) 'The Movement of the Squares in Greece: Symptom and Antidote to the Crisis of Democracy', *Actuel Marx*.

Papadimitropoulos, D. et al. (2011) 'From Bankruptcy to Self-recognition', *The Books' Journal*, no. 6, pp. 4–15.

Piketty, T. and Saez, E. (2003) 'Income Inequality in the United States, 1913–1998', *Quarterly Journal of Economics*, vol. 68, no. 1, pp. 1–37.

Pisani-Ferry, J. and Sapir, A. (2006) 'Last Exist to Lisbon', *Bruegel Policy Brief*, vol. 2, no. 2006/02, pp. 2–12.

Pizzorno, A. (1978) 'Political Exchange and Collective Identity in Industrial Conflict', Crouch, C. and Pizzorno, A. (eds), *The Resurgence of Class Conflict in W. Europe Since 1968*, Macmillan.

Polanyi, K. (1957 [1944]) *The Great Transformation: The Political and Economic Origins of Our Time*, Beacon Press.

Pollin, R. (2000) 'Globalization, Inequality and Financial Instability: Confronting the Marx, Keynes and Polanyi. Problems in Advanced Capitalist Economies', *PERI Working Papers Series*, no. 8, (http://works.bepress.com/robert_pollin/23, accessed May 2013).

Pollock, A. (2005) *NHS Plc: The Privatization of our Health Care*, Verso Books.

Porter, P. (1947) 'Wanted: A Miracle in Greece', *Collier's*, 9 September.

Poulantzas, N. (1980) *State, Power, Socialism*, Verso Books.

Putnam, R.D. (1993) *Making Democracy Work: Civil Traditions in Modern Italy*, Princeton University Press.

Quah, D. (1993) 'Empirical Cross-section Dynamics in Economic Growth', *European Economic Review*, vol. 37, no. 2/3, pp. 426–34.

Quiggin, J. (2000) 'Rent-seeking Industry Alive and Kicking', *Australian Financial Review*, 13 April (http://www.uq.edu.au/economics/johnquiggin/news00/Rent0004.html – accessed May 2013).

Quiggin, R. (2010) *Zombie Economics: How Dead Ideas Still Walk Among Us*, Princeton University Press.

Rajan, R. (2010) *Fault Lines: How Hidden Fractures Still Threaten the World Economy*, Princeton University Press.

Ramfos, S. (2011) *The Logic of Paranoia*, Armos (in Greek).

Reinhart, M. and Rogoff, D. (2009) *This Time is Different*, Princeton University Press.

Riley, D. (2012) 'Bernstein's Heirs', *New Left Review*, no. 76, pp. 136–50.

Rossanda, R. (2010) *The Comrade from Milan*, Verso books.

Rostow, W. (1971) *The Stages of Economic Growth: A Non-communist Manifesto*, Cambridge University Press.

Runciman, D. (2011) 'Didn't They Notice?', *London Review of Books*, vol. 33, no. 8, pp. 20–3.

Rylmon, P. (2011) 'There is No Quick Exit Strategy', *Epoxi*, 30 December.

Sachs, J. (2005) *The End of Poverty*, Penguin.

Seferiades, S. and Johnston, H. (2012) *Violent Protest, Contentious Politics, and the Neoliberal State*, Ashgate.

Shaw, P., Katsaiti, M-S. and Jurgilas, M. (2011) 'Corruption and Growth Under Weak Identification', *Economic Inquiry*, vol. 49, no. 1, pp. 264–75.

Shleifer, A. and Summers, L. (1988) 'Breach of Trust in Hostile Takeovers', in Auerbach, A.J. (ed.), *Corporate Takeovers: Causes and Consequences*, NBER, Chicago University Press.

Simigiannis, G.T. and Tzamourani, P.G. (2007) 'Borrowing and the Socio-economic Characteristics of Households', *Bank of Greece Economic Bulletin*, no. 28, pp. 31–49.

Simitis, K. (1989) *Development and Modernization of Greek Society*, Gnosi, Athens.

Skidelsky, R. (2011) 'Coordination vs. Disintegration', *The New Statesman*, 10 October (http://www.skidelskyr.com/site/article/coordination-vs-disintegration/ – accessed May 2013).

Stathakis, G. (2010) 'The Fiscal Crisis of the Greek Economy: A Historical Perspective', *Synchrona Themata*, no. 108, pp. 3–27.

Stiglitz, J. (1994) *Wither Socialism?* MIT Press.

Streeck, W. (1997) 'Beneficial Constraints: On the Economic Limits of Rational Voluntarism', in Rogers Hollingsworth, J. and Boyer, R. (eds), *Contemporary Capitalism: The Embeddedness of Institutions*, Cambridge University Press.

Streeck, W. (2011a) 'The Crises of Democratic Capitalism', *New Left Review*, no. 71, pp. 5–29.

Streeck, W. (2011b) 'Taking Capitalism Seriously: Towards an Institutionalist Approach to Contemporary Political Economy', *Socio-economic Review*, vol. 9, no. 1, pp. 137–67.

Streeck, W. (2012) 'Markets and Peoples: Democratic Capitalism and European Integration', *New Left Review*, no. 73, pp. 63–71.

Suchting, W.A. (1983) *Marx: An Introduction*, Wheatsheaf Books.

Svensson, J. (2005) 'Eight Questions about Corruption', *Journal of Economic Perspectives*, vol. 19, no. 3, pp. 19–42.

Tsakalotos, E. (1998) 'The Political Economy of Social Democratic Economic Policies: The PASOK Experiment in Greece', *Oxford Review of Economic Policy*, vol. 14, no. 1, pp. 114–38.

Tsakalotos, E. (2007) 'Competitive Equilibrium and the Social Ethos: Understanding the Inegalitarian Dynamics of Liberal Market Economies', *Politics and Society*, vol. 35, no. 3, pp. 427–46.

Tsakatika, M. (2007) 'Governance vs. Politics: The European Union's "Democratic Deficit"', *Journal of European Public Policy*, vol. 14, no. 6, pp. 867–85.

Turner, G. (2008) *Credit Crunch: Housing Bubbles, Globalisation and the Worldwide Economic Crisis*, Pluto Press.

Varoufakis, Y. (2011) *The Global Minotaur: America, the True Origins of the Financial Crisis and the Future of the World Economy*, Zed Books.

Varoufakis, Y. and Holland, S. (2012) 'A Modest Proposal for Resolving the Eurozone Crisis', *Intereconomics*, vol. 47, no. 4, pp. 240–47.

Varvaressos, K. (2002/1952) *Report on the Economic Problem in Greece*, Savalas (in Greek).

Wade, R. (1996) 'Japan, the World Bank and Art of Paradigm Maintenance: The East Asian Miracle in Political Perspective', *New Left Review*, no. 217, pp. 3–36.

Wolff, R. (2010) *Capitalism Hits the Fan: The Global Economic Meltdown and What to Do About It*, Olive Branch Press.

Wright, E.O. (2004) 'Beneficial Constraints: Beneficial for Whom?' *Socio-economic Review*, vol. 2, pp. 461–7.

Zhu, A., Ash, M. and Pollin, R. (2002) 'Stock Market Liquidity and Economic Growth: A Critical Appraisal of the Levine/Zervos Model', *Working Paper Series*, no. 47, Political Economy Research Institute, University of Massachusetts.

Index